*Dedicated in this 150th anniversary year
to the laypeople of
The Lutheran Church—Missouri Synod*

To the Ends of the Earth

A Journey through Acts

A. L. Barry

SAINT LOUIS

Copyright © 1997 Concordia Publishing House
3558 S. Jefferson Avenue, St. Louis, MO 63118-3968
Manufactured in the United States of America

Library of Congress Cataloging-in-Publication Data

Barry, A. L., 1931–
    To the ends of the earth: a journey through Acts / A. L. Barry.
        p.   cm.
    Includes bibliographical references.
    ISBN 0-570-04985-7
    1. Bible. N. T. Acts—Criticism, interpretation, etc. 2. Bible—Use. I. Title.
    BS2625.2.B35   1997
    226.6'06--dc21
                                                                            97-6400

---

1 2 3 4 5 6 7 8 9 10   06 05 04 03 02 01 00 99 98 97

Acknowledgments

It is always nice to be able to express gratitude. That is my happy privilege, for this book is indebted to many people. I have been delighted that so many have thought this kind of journey through Acts a worthwhile effort. In several ways they extended themselves to lend a hand. Any problems or faults herein are my responsibility.

First, a word of special thanks to the Rev. Kenneth Schurb, one of my staff assistants. His help in both the research and preparation of this book has been much appreciated.

Next, let me mention several congregations and pastors of The Lutheran Church—Missouri Synod. These churches served as field-test sites for much of the material eventually incorporated into this book: Immanuel Lutheran Church, Olivette, Missouri (Pastors Ray Mirly and Paul Rueckert); Immanuel Lutheran Church, Spirit Lake, Iowa (Pastor Phill Andreasen); and Zion Lutheran Church, Fort Wayne, Indiana (Pastors Matthew Harrison and Paul Kaiser). Their reactions proved most valuable.

Dr. Harold Buls, professor emeritus of Concordia Theological Seminary, Fort Wayne, Indiana, served as a "theological consultant" to this project. He read each chapter and submitted comments based on his experience as a teacher of the New Testament in general and of Acts in particular.

Others who helped include two professors from Concordia University, Irvine, California. Professor Robert Dargatz made insightful remarks on the manuscript and Dr. Thomas Doyle gave suggestions for the discussion questions. Dr. Paul Grime of the Synod's Commission on Worship also provided recommendations on portions of the book and some of the questions. Dr. Karl Barth, director of the Synod's 150th anniversary celebration, not only offered suggestions on the book but also contributed the foreword.

My thanks to the editor of the *Concordia Historical Institute Quarterly* for permitting me to repeat some thoughts from my article, "Church History and the Spiritual Formation of the People of God," (*CHIQ* 69, 1) in chapter 1. Thanks also to the CPH editor, Dawn Weinstock, who encouraged the "travel" format that marks the following pages.

I would be remiss if I did not acknowledge my great debt to and love for a special person over the years and during the time when this book was taking shape. I am referring, of course, to a very courageous and wonderful woman, my dear wife, Jean, who has since gone home to be with the Lord.

Finally, to the triune God, who daily graces our lives with His presence and blessings, forever be thanks and praise. *Soli Deo gloria!*

Dr. A. L. Barry
Epiphany 1997

Contents

ABBREVIATIONS

Essays—C.F.W. Walther. *Essays for the Church.* 2 vols. St. Louis: Concordia, 1992.

Hoyer—Theodore Hoyer, "Missionary Forward Movement in the Light of the Book of Acts." *Proceedings of the Seventeenth Convention of the Southern Illinois District of the Ev. Luther. Synod of Missouri, Ohio, and Other States assembled at Belleville, Illinois, October 15–19, 1934.* St. Louis: Concordia, 1934.

Janzow—*Luther's Large Catechism: A Contemporary Translation with Study Questions.* Tr. by F. Samuel Janzow. St. Louis: Concordia, 1978. (References following the Janzow page number refer to the *Large Catechism* portion of the *Book of Concord.*)

LT—Dietrich Bonhoeffer. *Life Together.* Tr. by John W. Doberstein. New York: Harper and Row, 1954.

LW—*Luther's Works.* American Edition. Gen. eds. Jaroslav Pelikan and Helmut Lehman. 55 vols. St. Louis and Philadelphia: Concordia and Fortress, 1955–86.

Tappert—Theodore G. Tappert, ed. *The Book of Concord.* Philadelphia: Muhlenberg, 1959. (References following the Tappert page number refer to portions of the *Book of Concord.*)

Unless otherwise noted, all biblical translations are "homemade."

Foreword

The book of Acts "is not the story of Paul as much as it is the story of Jesus continuing to proclaim His Word through the church."

With these words Dr. Barry sets the tone for this helpful little volume. He reminds us that a journey through Acts should do much more than rehearse how the early church witnessed "to the ends of the earth." It should—and this journey does—apply the earlier witness to *our* mission and ministry.

The author serves as our "tour guide" in a pastoral way. His words on handling conflict between Christians (*a la* Paul and Barnabas, for example) are worth reading more than once, as is the pattern he offers the church today from the story of the apostolic council. When he speaks of the importance of prayer or of the means of grace or of the pastor's responsibility to be faithful, we hear the beating of an undershepherd's heart.

The style is conversational. It is simple, practical, and clear. The personal anecdotes from family travels in the Winnebago travel trailer and from rich parish experience add to the pleasure.

Most important, at the heart of this book is the Gospel of God's grace and mercy in Jesus Christ given freely to sinners. That Gospel permeates the entire volume and is the basis for all applications to the life of the church. And while this work is dedicated to the laypeople of the church, it is hoped that pastors too will be reminded through it that our task is to "know nothing except Jesus Christ and Him crucified."

More than once we are told that Acts is "an open-ended account so the rest of His story—all the way down to us—can fit in." During this 150th anniversary year of The Lutheran Church—Missouri Synod, we, as people *sent forth by God's blessing*, see our story too as an "open-ended account" to be completed only when He comes.

Karl L. Barth
President Emeritus,
Concordia Seminary, St. Louis, Missouri

Introduction

In 1966, while serving as a parish pastor in southern Minnesota, my wife, Jean, and I decided to purchase a Winnebago travel trailer. We felt it was a good investment, especially since our children were young and we could use it for family vacations and occasional two- or three-day getaways.

I must confess that shortly after we purchased the Winnebago, I had some misgivings about the financial wisdom of our purchase of the new vehicle. But in 1992, when we finally sold it, there was no question that it had been a good investment. We could look back at many vacations, both with the children and after they left home, when we had gone places and done things that, without the travel trailer, I know we never would have done.

Journeying in the Word

Eighteen years ago, I committed myself to travel of a different sort. I decided that, in addition to my daily devotions, I would read through the entire Scriptures from beginning to end once every year.

While I had done significant Bible reading prior to this decision, I had never adopted this particular goal. Over the years, my annual trips through God's Word from stem to stern certainly have taken time. But I quickly add: What a blessing these journeys have been!

A Journey through Acts

Now, I would like you to join me in an adventure. Together, we will journey through one of the most action-filled books of the Bible—Acts. This exciting portion of Scripture describes the very earliest days of the Christian church after Jesus rose from the dead and ascended into heaven. Acts often has been called the first "church history."

The human author of Acts was the "beloved physician" (Colossians 4:14) and traveling companion of the apostle Paul—Luke. (See the "we" sections: Acts 16:10–17; 20:5–16; 21:1–18; 27:1–28:31.) By inspiration of the Holy Spirit, Luke wrote Acts, along with the gospel that bears his name, probably in the early- to mid-60s A.D. Already in Luke 1:1–4 it becomes plain to the reader that Luke was a methodical person who, under the Spirit's guidance, did meticulous research and detailed writing. We will notice that same high level of organization in Acts.

We have not tried to set up this study in the customary Bible study format. I want to approach our reading of Acts as a trip we take together. And I would like to think of this trip more as a beginning than as an ending, both for you and for me. I hope you will read through Acts again and again, and go on to other books of the Bible. It is important that we dive regularly into the Word.

According to an old saying, "Give someone a fish and you feed him for a day. Teach him to fish and you feed him for a lifetime." As we travel through Acts, you will learn and practice some ideas that you can use in your ongoing Bible reading and study. In fact, you can apply these concepts as you read other books.

In the first half of our journey, I will suggest principles that can be applied to anything you read, including the Bible. The second half will include ideas to help you read sections of the Bible that tell stories. These accounts often are called "narratives." I think you will find this emphasis on developing your reading skills to be a unique feature of our trip together.

Throughout the journey, make use of the discussion questions in the back of this book. You can use them by yourself or in a class setting. These questions will help you focus on God's Word and apply the reading skills we will discuss.

Navigational Helps

When we travel, we study the atlas or map and carefully plot our route. As we do so, we keep in mind what the symbols mean. Otherwise, our trip may be delayed unnecessarily as we travel side streets instead of major roads.

Just as understanding and remembering visual terminology helps you read a map, understanding and remembering the following terminology will help you maintain your bearings as you read this book.

1. Whenever I refer to "the book," this means the book you are now reading, *not* Acts.

2. Whenever you encounter the word "chapter"

beyond this sentence, it refers to a chapter of this book, *not* to one of the 28 chapters of Acts.

3. Bible references in parentheses that do not specify a book of the Bible refer to passages in Acts.

Record Your Impressions

When we took family vacations in the Winnebago, we sent postcards to family and friends. On occasion, the recipients would show us one of these cards, sometimes years after the trip. What fun it was to look at the pictures and recall the real sites. But I found it even more meaningful to read the messages on the back of the cards. Here we had recorded, in our own words, what we had seen and experienced in our travels.

You can record your impressions as we travel through Acts. Just jot a note in the margins of your Bible, in this book, or keep a "travel" notebook. In fact, as I prepared to serve as your tour guide through Acts, I enjoyed the opportunity to add still more notations to the margins of my Bible. I encourage you never to hesitate to write in your Bible as you read. And it is my prayer that you will, at some point in the future, delight in reading what you wrote while you took this particular journey.

A Great Blessing

Finally, before we start, let us pause and reflect on what a tremendous blessing it is to be able to read, learn, and "inwardly digest" the verbally inspired

Word of God, whether individually or as a Bible study group member. I marvel when I think of how the Lord took a man like St. Luke and used his background, his intellect, his writing style, and even his historical research to bring about a text that is entirely His Word—a text that is totally reliable, without error, and has the power of God Himself to bless, help, and save us in our Lord Jesus Christ.

> The things that were written previously [in the Scriptures] were written for our instruction, in order that we might have hope through the comfort which the Scriptures give us. *(Romans 15:4)*

The adventure awaits, as does the blessing. Soon we will have the trailer hooked up. Then we will climb in the car and head out. Can you feel the anticipation?

May the Lord be with us and bless us as we journey through Acts!

PART I:SUGGESTIONS FOR READING ANY BOOK

Section A

Pay Attention to the Beginning and the Ending

I enjoy remembering some of our extended vacations in the Winnebago. As I reflect, these trips always involved three stages. First, we got ready. Second was the trip itself. The third stage began when we returned home. It included unpacking the trailer and talking again and again about all the places we had been, the things we had done, and the people we had seen.

Our vacations really were more than just the time on the road. Without the first stage—the preparation—the trip would not have occurred. And once we returned home, we couldn't omit unpacking or reminiscing. Beginnings and endings framed our travels.

Just as beginnings and endings are important when we travel, they also are important when we read. As we take our trip through Acts, we should give due attention to the very beginning. And we also need to peek ahead to the end. Based on this, our first piece of advice for reading urges us to *pay attention to the beginning and the ending.*

The better organized the book, the more helpful you will find this principle. Organized writers like St. Luke generally tell you what they're going to tell you, then tell you, and finally, tell you what they told you. In modern books, prefaces, forewords, content lists, and even dust jackets inform us of what we might encounter within. I am even told that readers of mystery novels sometimes read the conclusion first so they can better enjoy the suspense and plot twists to come.

Although Acts has no preface, content list, or foreword, we can benefit from examining its beginning and its ending. Chapter 1 will deal with the very first and last sentences of Acts. Chapters 2 and 3 will discuss two fantastic realities in the Christian faith: the ascension of our Lord and Pentecost. Both events are described at the beginning of Acts.

Chapter 1

The Continuation Continued

Read Acts 1:1–3; 28:30–31

If we want to pay attention to the very beginning and the very end of Acts, we will look at its very first and very last sentences. On a long journey like the one before us, this may amount to no more than pulling out of the driveway. But such a start should not be underestimated. Without it, the rest of the trip will not go nearly as well as it could. Thus, we look at the opening sentence of Acts.

> O Theophilus, in my first book I wrote about all the things which Jesus began to do and to teach until the day He was taken up after having given instructions through the Holy Spirit to His chosen apostles, to whom He showed Himself alive after His suffering by many convincing proofs, being seen by them for 40 days and speaking the things about the kingdom of God. *(1:1–3)*

And here is the concluding sentence of Acts, which tells us about the apostle Paul.

> For two whole years he remained in his own rented place, and received all those who came in to him, preaching the kingdom of God and teaching the things about the Lord Jesus Christ with all boldness, unhindered. *(28:30–31)*

Asking the Five *Ws*

Let's put a few simple questions to these beginning and ending sentences.

WHO? The first sentence of Acts mentions several people. But mainly it focuses on the crucified, risen, and about-to-ascend Lord Jesus Christ. The last sentence of Acts discusses the apostle Paul.

WHERE? Acts 1 mentions Jesus' death and resurrection, which we know took place in Jerusalem. It also mentions "all the things which Jesus began to do and teach," which would have taken us to Galilee and the Ten Towns—sites in Palestine. In Acts 28 Paul is in Rome. We might say that he was on his fourth missionary journey. Unlike the previous three, however, this was an all-expense-paid trip courtesy of the Roman Empire! Paul had come to Rome as a prisoner, and he now found himself under house arrest in the capital city.

WHEN? The Acts 1 passage mentions the 40 days of teaching Jesus did between His resurrection and ascension. Acts 28 says that Paul remained under house arrest for two years. Then the account simply ends without saying what happened next.

WHAT? What was going on? Our sentences tell us that Jesus and Paul both taught about the kingdom of God. I have always liked that phrase. A concise, helpful definition can be found in Martin Luther's *Large Catechism*. It says the kingdom of God is

> that God sent His Son, our Lord Christ, into
> the world to redeem us and set us free from
> the power of the devil and to bring us to

Himself and rule over us as a king of right-eousness, life, and salvation in defiance of sin, death, and an evil conscience. *(Janzow, p. 86; LC III 51)*

It is no accident in the gospels that, as Jesus died, there were more reminders than at any other time that He is the King. Just think of the sign on the cross, the crown of thorns, the taunts from the crowd direct-ed at the "king." On the cross the humble yet almighty King, Jesus, was procuring His kingdom. He paid for it with His lifeblood.

Nor is it an accident that the end of Acts notes that Paul was "preaching the kingdom of God" and "teaching the things about the Lord Jesus Christ." To talk about the kingdom is to talk about Christ. (See 8:12; 20:24–25; 28:23.)

Finally, we arrive at the biggest question. **WHY** were these things being done? In Acts 1 Luke recalls the first book he wrote to Theophilus, the gospel of Luke, and comments, "I wrote about all the things which Jesus *began* to do and to teach" (emphasis added). The Master's birth, His baptism, His preach-ing, His healing, His miracles, His compassion, His parables, His prayers, His journey to Jerusalem, His death and rising from the dead—that was all in Luke's first book. But it was just the beginning.

The events in Acts are themselves a clue to why Luke wrote the book. He was writing the second vol-ume—Acts—to report what Jesus *kept on* doing and teaching. This remains the focus of Acts down to its final sentence, where we find Paul preaching the kingdom of God.

And this returns us to the beginning of our questions. Perhaps we were a bit hasty in answering **WHO.** Not only is *Paul's* preaching described in Acts 28, more significantly, this proclamation of the kingdom is *Christ's* work. Not only does the first sentence of Acts concentrate on the activity of Jesus, but the last one does too as the ascended Lord continues His work through an apostle like Paul. Ultimately, we find in our study of the first and last sentences that Acts is the continuation of the story about Jesus that Luke started in the "first book," his gospel. And this continuation in Acts is itself continued in our preaching and teaching the kingdom of God today.

Lessons from the Beginning and Ending of Acts

When reading the Scriptures, it's good to ask the basic observation questions: *who, where, when, what,* and *why.* But what have we learned from putting these questions to the first and last sentences of Acts? I believe we can take away important information about Acts, Jesus, and ourselves.

Information about Acts

By paying attention to the beginning and ending, we can see why Acts has what some readers might consider an unsatisfactory ending. True, the last sentence does not tell us what happened after Paul's two years under house arrest, but what difference does that make? Acts is not the story of Paul as much as it is the story of Jesus continuing to proclaim His Word through His church.

Let me repeat that thought. *Acts is the story of Jesus continuing to proclaim His Word through His church.* It is an open-ended account so the rest of His story—all the way down to us—can fit in.

Information about Jesus

Make no mistake, the work of proclaiming the Gospel remains Christ's. The story of Jesus continues today because He is still doing and teaching, still establishing His kingdom among people by His powerful Word. As the *Large Catechism* says, "To be baptized in God's name is to be baptized not by man but by God Himself" (Janzow, p. 99; LC IV 10).

This fact takes a lot of pressure off us. Christ works through us, but He does not depend on us. We depend on Him and as we do, He mightily blesses.

Information about Ourselves

When our children were growing up, I took special care to share this biblical account of Christ and His kingdom with them. Now, I am eager to share it with our grandchildren. Why? Because this is exciting! You and I *do* fit into the story! Unworthy, guilty sinners that we are, Jesus died for us too. By the grace of God, you and I have a place in the story because we have a place under the cross. By the grace of God, the work of the church—pastors and people—in proclaiming the kingdom forms part of this story.

We are positioned by our good and gracious God to enjoy in Christ all the eternal blessings of salvation from sin, death, and an evil conscience. And we are positioned to share the story with others so they too will enjoy a place under the cross.

Christ Himself came to be a light to the Gentiles as well as the glory of Israel (Luke 2:32; Acts 26:23). As we in the church tell His message—that is, as Christ continues to work through us—we too are "a light of the Gentiles for salvation to the ends of the earth" (13:47).

Chapter 2

Not Gone and Not Forgotten

Read Acts 1:1–12

In chapter 1, we did not go beyond the first sentence and the last sentence of Acts. Truly, the Lord has vast riches in store for us between these two sentences. It is to some of these riches that we will move in this second chapter. But even in this chapter, we will not penetrate too far into Acts 1. We will focus on a specific event: the ascension of our Lord.

Pride of Place: The Ascension

If you look at the last four verses of the gospel according to St. Luke, you find that Acts begins precisely where Luke's first book ended—the ascension (Luke 24:50–53). It must be a major event.

At His ascension, Jesus was lifted up from the

earth. When the apostles could no longer see Him, two angels ("men in white clothes" in Acts) told them that He would come back in the same way they had seen Him go (1:9–11).

The ascension is one of two events that enjoys pride of place in Acts. The other is Pentecost, the subject of chapter 3. These two events set the tone for the rest of Acts, just as they set the tone for the lives of the apostles and others in the first-century church.

Don't Misunderstand Jesus' Departure

Unfortunately, the tone set by the ascension and Pentecost is often misunderstood. One of the great myths about Acts is that it is the "Gospel of the Holy Spirit"—that it records what happened after Jesus supposedly left the earth at His ascension. According to this faulty idea, the Holy Spirit came to the church as a divine substitute for the departed and absent Son.

This myth is tempting because it contains a slight element of truth. As we shall see, Acts does have a great deal to say about the Holy Spirit. And Jesus did promise to send the Holy Spirit after He ascended into heaven (1:4–5; see John 14:15–17; 16:7). But in light of the conclusion we reached in chapter 1—that Acts continues the story of Jesus—we should resist any suggestion that Jesus is somehow absent from His people in Acts. Such a suggestion stands on two wobbly legs: faulty ideas about what the ascension means in Acts and, more generally, faulty ideas about who Jesus is.

Upon such wobbly legs, conclusions can be built

such as that in the New International Version translation of Acts 3:21. The original Greek text of Acts mentions the ascended Christ, "whom it is necessary for heaven to receive." But the NIV goes far beyond this, saying, "He must *remain* in heaven" (emphasis added). The assumption behind this translation seems to be that a human body can be in only one place at a time. Thus, it would follow that after the ascension Jesus *cannot* be present on earth according to His human nature. (In this discussion, we should recognize that no Bible translation is perfect. It's helpful, therefore, to compare English versions. Among those recommended for close study are the New American Standard Bible [NASB] and the New Evangelical Translation [NET, formerly called the "God's Word to the Nations" translation or GWN]. This underlines the necessity of training future pastors in the biblical languages so they can evaluate Bible translations against the original Greek or Hebrew text.)

Such a false conclusion has broad impact, even beyond how people look at the ascension. Through the years, it also has affected doctrinal positions concerning Communion. It has been the reason lurking behind the denial by some denominations of the real presence of Christ's body and blood in His Supper. Beginning with the assumption that the body of our Lord *cannot* be present in more than one place at a time, people reason that it cannot be in heaven and also present on the altar in uncounted churches. Historically, denial of Christ's real presence in the Lord's Supper has been a symptom of further doctrinal problems about subjects such as the person of Christ.

Christ *Is* Present with His Church

In Acts the misconception that Christ is no longer present never comes up—except in mistranslations of Acts 3:21! On the contrary, as Acts depicts the ascended Lord, we find that Jesus repeatedly manifests Himself on earth.

- On the road to Damascus, Christ appeared to Saul, later called Paul (9:3–5). This was probably the occasion to which Paul referred in writing to the Corinthians: "Last of all ... He [Jesus] was seen also by me" (1 Corinthians 15:8; see 1 Corinthians 9:1).

- Christ's continuing presence with His church is described in Acts 14:3, where the "Lord" (Jesus, in the language of the early church, see John 21:7; Acts 1:6; Acts 2:36; Acts 9:17; 1 Corinthians 6:14; 1 Corinthians 12:3; 2 Corinthians 4:5; 2 Corinthians 13:14) testified to His Word of grace by working signs and wonders through the hands of Paul and Barnabas.

- In Acts 18:9–10, the same Lord appeared to Paul in a vision. He had a message identical to the one He had given the disciples earlier, "I am with you" (Matthew 28:20).

- Finally, we read about the events of the night after Paul's appearance before the Sanhedrin following his arrest in Jerusalem. The Lord not only appeared to the apostle but *stood near him,* assuring Paul that he would bring the Gospel to Rome (23:11).

In these and other passages, Acts—which begins with Christ's ascension—indicates the continuing presence of Jesus with His church as it spreads His Word. Indeed, Acts tells us what Jesus kept on doing and teaching (1:1). The ascended Lord is not confined simply to a place in heaven! He is still very much present with His church on earth, present even when He is not visible.

We can reinforce this point if we pay attention to the ending of two other biblical books. Let's briefly compare the ending of Matthew with the ending of Luke. The end of Luke tells the story of the ascension—how Jesus was taken up into heaven and the apostles praised God (Luke 24:50–53). The end of Matthew includes the Great Commission and Jesus' promise, "I am with you always, even to the end of the age" (Matthew 28:20).

These two endings show us two sides of the one reality of Jesus' ascension. Although the ascended Lord is not visibly present anywhere on earth, He is invisibly present with us everywhere (Ephesians 1:20–23). The gospel according to St. Luke hones in on the visible aspect while the gospel according to St. Matthew stresses the invisible, ongoing presence of Christ.

This point also is reflected in the High Priestly Prayer that Jesus prayed just hours before His crucifixion. He said, "I am no longer in the world" (John 17:11) and "I have made Your name known to them and *I will make it known*" (John 17:26, emphasis added).

The Person of Christ

The belief that Jesus is gone from the earth after

the ascension is clearly false. Not only is such a belief based on a misconception about what the ascension means, it also rests on another wobbly leg—a misconception about the person of Christ.

In truth, Jesus *can* be invisibly present with us everywhere, even according to His human nature. The divine and human natures are so closely united in this unique person of Christ that the human nature receives divine powers (sometimes called *attributes*) from the divine nature. The *Formula of Concord* explains it well.

> To give life, to execute all judgment, to have all authority in heaven and on earth, to have all things given into His hands, to have all things under His feet, to cleanse from sin, and so forth are ... divine and infinite qualities. Yet according to the statement of the Scriptures these properties have been given and communicated to the man Christ. (The *Formula of Concord* cites John 5:21, 27; 6:39, 40; Matthew 28:18; Daniel 7:14; John 3:31, 35; 13:3; Matthew 11:27; Ephesians 1:22; Hebrews 2:8; 1 Corinthians 15:27; John 1:3, 10.) *(Tappert, p. 601; FC SD VIII 54)*

Why is this so important? We find the answer later in the *Formula of Concord*. The confessors describe the importance of this teaching in our Christian lives in an inviting manner. They write that

> ... according to and with this same assumed human nature of His, Christ can be and is present wherever He wills, and in particular

that He is present with His church and community on earth as mediator, head, king, and high priest. Not part or only one-half of the person of Christ, but the entire person to which both natures, the divine and the human, belong is present. He is present not only according to His deity, but also according to and with His assumed human nature, according to which He is our brother and we flesh of His flesh and bone of His bone (Ephesians 5:30). To make certainty and assurance doubly sure on this point, He instituted His Holy Supper that He might be present with us, dwell in us, work and be mighty in us according to that nature, too, according to which He has flesh and blood. *(Tappert, pp. 606–607; FC SD VIII 78–79)*

Christ's ascension provides the backdrop for the entire book of Acts. This backdrop does not feature an absentee Lord but a Jesus who is very much present with and active in His church. He is the Christ who promised His people that

not only His unveiled deity, which to us poor sinners is like a consuming fire on dry stubble, will be with them, but that He, He, the man who has spoken with them, who has tasted every tribulation in His assumed human nature, and who can therefore sympathize with us as with men and His brethren, *He* wills to be with us in all our troubles also according to that nature by which He is our brother and we are flesh of

His flesh. *(Tappert, p. 608, emphasis added; FC SD VIII 87)*

When a great leader or a close friend dies, we often hear people say that the person is gone but not forgotten. As we read Acts together, we find that the ascended Christ is not forgotten by His church nor is He gone. This fact is as true and comforting for us today as it was in the first century. It gives us comfort and courage in life and also when we face the loss of a loved one in death. Thanks be to God for this great truth found in His Spirit-given Word in Acts!

Chapter 3

The Pentecost Phenomenon

Read Acts 2:1–41

After Christ's ascension, the second big event that occurs early in Acts is Pentecost. Like the ascension, Pentecost helps set the tone for what follows. Thus, we focus on the Acts 2 account of Pentecost as we note the beginning and the ending of Acts.

Ingathering at Pentecost

That great Pentecost day began and ended with the Word of God. The Christians spoke in languages they had not previously learned so a wide variety of Jewish festival pilgrims from numerous places, including towns in Africa and Europe, heard about the mighty acts of God in their native tongue (2:4–11). The Lord who had confused the language of people at the Tower of Babel (Genesis 11:1–9) was now taking the initiative to effect unity among speakers of different languages.

Of course, the members of the crowd would have understood languages such as Aramaic or Greek so the miraculous powers of speech given at Pentecost were not necessary to communicate. Something more was afoot.

The Lord had long promised to gather all nations *and tongues* (Isaiah 66:18). The Pentecost phenomenon will reach its fullness in heaven, where God's people—the great multitude from every nation, tribe, people, and language—will stand before the throne and before the Lamb (Revelation 7:9). The Lord was not bringing His people together at Pentecost around a single common language, but around His Word and around Himself and His gift of salvation. As Martin Luther said, "God's Word cannot be without God's people" (LW vol. 41, p. 150).

Word and Spirit

God's Word was also in evidence in other ways on this red-letter Pentecost day. In fact, wherever the crowd turned on Pentecost they were bumping into God's Word. In his sermon, the apostle Peter quoted from the Old Testament, citing what the Lord had said through His spokesmen Joel the prophet (2:17–21) and David the king (2:25–28, 34–35). Even the miraculous *"tongues* as of flame" (2:3, emphasis added) remind us of speech and of proclaiming the Word! Finally, at the end of Peter's sermon comes the application of water and the Word to people in Baptism (2:38–41; see Ephesians 5:25–27).

The same Lord Jesus who 50 days earlier on the first Easter had *breathed* on His disciples and *said*, "Receive the Holy Spirit" (John 20:22) was continuing to send out His Spirit with His Word. He still does. By this Word the Pentecost crowd certainly caught the Spirit—the Holy Spirit. About three thousand were added to the church on that day alone (2:41).

The Church's Birthday?

Pentecost sometimes has been called the "birthday of the Christian church." This is not a bad nickname, as long as we remember that many had believed in the promised Christ even before He came in the flesh.

The Last Days

In his sermon, Peter helped his hearers understand what was occurring. He quoted the Word of God from the prophecy of Joel and characterized it as a passage about the "last days."

Peter could use this phrase because once the work of redemption was accomplished, everything after is the last days. The Lord spoke to our fathers by the prophets, the New Testament says, but now *in these last days* He has spoken to us by His Son who is His last and best message to sinners (Hebrews 1:1–2;

1 Peter 1:20). Anyone claiming to have a newer or better word from God is, in effect, saying that the Savior is not the last word. But He is. That is what the Gospel is all about. In Christ, all the promises of God find their "yes" and "amen" (2 Corinthians 1:20).

Many people say that we live in the last days, and we do. But some fail to notice that we have been in the last days since Pentecost! The term "last days" refers both to *quantity* and to *quality* of time. The end of the world, mentioned in Joel (2:19–20 quoting Joel 2:30–31), is the next and final great thing that the Creator will accomplish on the stage of world history.

The Pentecost phenomenon will come to its fullness in the resurrection of the dead and the life of the world to come. We await this, just as Old Testament era believers awaited Christ's first coming. While Pentecost is the birthday of the Christian church, and as such it has to do with beginnings, it also lifts our heads and points us to the end when the Lord will take His people home.

The Pentecost Phenomenon

What is the Pentecost phenomenon? Joel says in these last days the Lord would pour out His Spirit on all flesh so everyone who calls on His name will be saved (2:17, 21 quoting Joel 2:28–29, 32). This is the Pentecost phenomenon.

On that remarkable Pentecost day, the Spirit was poured out visibly and audibly. Acts 2:17–18 points out that in the New Testament era the Holy Spirit would go out far and wide, touching old and young, men and women, as the message of Christ went out far and wide. These verses emphasize the proclamation of the Word (note the word *prophesy*) by mentioning it twice.

Indeed, the Bible continually urges Christians to "let Christ's word live richly among [us], as [we] teach and admonish each other with all wisdom, singing psalms, hymns, and spiritual songs to God in [our] thankful hearts" (Colossians 3:16). When the Holy Spirit works, God's Word not only finds a place in our hearts, but also on our lips.

The Spirit at Work: Proclaiming Christ

Above all, the Holy Spirit calls attention to Christ (John 14:26; 15:26; 16:14). About two-thirds of Peter's sermon was devoted to talking specifically about the Master (2:22–36).

Peter said that God attested to Jesus through miracles, wonderful proofs, and signs and that at length He was vindicated by God in His resurrection. Still, it had been God's plan that Jesus would be betrayed and killed (2:23), although He did not deserve it. He was the Lamb of God, bearing the sin of the world (John 1:29), and eventually He died under its weight. He had to die, not for His sin but for ours.

In view of His empty tomb, though, it is clear that "God has made Him Lord and Christ" (2:36). Peter proclaimed that Jesus, the Lord exalted to God's right hand, was the one who poured out the Holy Spirit in this marvelous way (2:33–35).

The Spirit at Work: Getting Personal

The Holy Spirit got personal. Peter spoke to the crowd of "this Jesus whom *you* crucified" (2:36, emphasis added; see 2:23). Remember, many of these people were pilgrims from far-flung places. Even if they had been present in Jerusalem seven weeks earlier for the Passover, how many of them would have been in the crowd that shouted, "Crucify Him"? Nonetheless, on that Pentecost day Peter referred to the Jesus "whom *you* crucified."

Peter could do the same thing if he preached at your church or mine. Because Jesus bore all the sin of all people of all time, He also died for your sin and mine. Our sins put Him on the cross just as much as anyone else's.

Just like the Pentecost crowd, we should react to this reality like people who have been cut with a knife. Even today the Word of God is that sharp, if not sharper (Hebrews 4:12). When it exposes our sin, we find ourselves saying, as Peter's audience cried out, "What shall we do?" (2:37). And for us, as in their case, the Good News lies in the forgiveness of sins brought to us in Baptism and in the Word, which confer on us the gift of the Holy Spirit (2:38).

Exactly What We Need

Salesmen talk about the point of sale; educators speak of delivery systems. No matter what you are trying to provide to people, it must be distributed if it is to help them. Like all sinners, we need the blessing of salvation on account of Christ. And the Holy Spirit brings us this blessing. Martin Luther put it this way in the *Large Catechism:*

> Christ has purchased and won the treasure for us through His suffering, death, resurrection, etc. But if that saving action stays hidden and no one knows about it, then it would all be for nothing, wasted. In order that this treasure might not remain buried but be taken up and enjoyed, God has let the Word go forth and be proclaimed. In the Word He has given us His Holy Spirit to lay the treasure of redemption on our hearts and make it our very own. *(Janzow, p. 73; LC II 38)*

This is exactly what we need. We have sins that only Christ can forgive, and the Spirit brings Him to us through God's Word. We need fellowship with God and with others, and the Spirit gives us fellowship by calling and gathering us into the Lord's church. We need hope because the final judgment awaits us (sooner than we think) in these last days, and the Spirit comforts us with the assurance that the Pentecost phenomenon ends in rejoicing before the throne of God and of the Lamb.

A Look Ahead

The account of Pentecost, positioned early in Acts, in some ways gives us a sneak peek. As our journey through Acts continues, we will see the Holy Spirit setting into motion again and again the proclamation of the crucified, risen, and ascended Lord

Jesus. As in Acts 2, these proclamations often are connected with a miraculous event in the apostolic church. We also will see faithful proclaimers repeatedly meeting with mockers. And we will observe how the church grew, even in unlikely places and under unlikely circumstances.

The Two Dimensions of Pentecost

For believers in Christ, the Pentecost phenomenon has two dimensions. First, the ascended Christ has poured out His Spirit on us so we, calling on the name of the Lord, are saved. But Pentecost also challenges us to reach out to others with the Good News. This is its second dimension. Thus, the Pentecost phenomenon goes through us to others by the power of the Holy Spirit. Thanks be to God for this great blessing in Christ.

Section B

Pay Attention to Internal Organization

As we move ahead in our journey through Acts, we will stop along the way to point out some general principles to apply to Bible study. You can use these in your Bible reading even after you finish this particular journey. So far we have been applying the suggestion *pay attention to the beginning and the ending.*

As I already have mentioned, beginnings and endings are important as we travel and as we read. As I think back to our days in the family travel trailer, I also remember that even before we ventured out on the open road, we had a family discussion about where we wanted to travel and what items we wanted to see. It always seemed there were more things we wanted to do and more places we wanted to go than there was time. Finally, we simply looked at the map and made some selections, trying to satisfy at least one thing on everyone's "I-want-to-see-that" list.

As the date of our departure drew closer and

closer, you probably can imagine how our anticipation grew. We knew where we were going, and we were excited and anxious to get there.

Knowing where we were going also helped us after we started out. We knew that we would see the mountains before we saw the ocean. We could anticipate what was ahead at each stage of the trip.

This same idea applies when we read. Whether reading Acts or any other book in the Bible, we need to *pay attention to internal organization*. This applies to anything we read, even the newspaper. All authors organize their work, some more strictly and tightly than others. Good writers find ways to clue in the reader to their organizational plans so the reader becomes aware of what to expect.

Acts—inspired by the Holy Spirit to be written through the orderly mind of the learned physician Luke—is a well-organized account. We will observe this feature of Acts in our next three chapters. First, we will note that Acts offers a general organizational statement. Then we will follow this organizational plan as the narrative moves ahead. Knowing where we are going always makes the trip more satisfying.

Chapter 4

Witnesses?

Read Acts 1:8, 13–26

Paying attention to the internal organization of what we read helps us learn where we are going. It's like having a road map. As we read Acts, we find that this is an apt comparison.

Almost immediately, Acts gives us an insight into its organization. It turns out that this organization is, in large measure, geographic. We actually can plot it on a map. Just before His ascension, Jesus said, "But you will receive power when the Holy Spirit has come upon you, and you will be my witnesses in Jerusalem, and in all Judea and Samaria, and to the ends of the earth" (1:8).

This verse forms something of an outline for Acts, though Acts does not tell us everything that occurred in these places. The action in Acts 1:1–7:45 happened in Jerusalem. In Acts 8:1–12:25, we see the Gospel moving into Judea and Samaria. And the latter half of Acts (13:1–28:31), takes us into all the world as we follow the journeys of Paul.

Eyewitnesses

Acts 1:8 provides more than a road map, helpful as that is. Here, Jesus briefly indicates the capacity in which the apostles would leave the mount of ascension and go forth to serve in the locations He mentioned. They would be witnesses. This is a key word in Acts, and one which we still use a great deal today. However, it may come as a surprise that we cannot claim to be witnesses to Christ in the same way Acts uses the term to describe Christ's early followers.

In Acts, *witness* means *eyewitness*. And the word *eyewitnesses* precisely describes what the apostles were. At any time they could be hauled into a court of law to offer firsthand testimony about Jesus of Nazareth, not hearsay. And this is what happened. When the Jewish council ordered Peter and John not to speak in the name of Jesus, Peter said, "We are not able not to speak of the things *which we have seen and heard*" (4:20, emphasis added). Clearly, Peter was not making the Gospel what *he* wanted it to be. Instead, he was reporting what God had done in Christ.

The same point emerges in the second half of Acts 1 when the apostles sought a replacement for Judas. Peter said it was necessary for this person to be a *witness* of Jesus' resurrection. More than that, Peter also talked about the need to select someone from among the *men* (he used the Greek word for *males*) who had been with them during the whole time that the Lord Jesus went in and out among them (1:20–22).

This emphasis on eyewitness testimony is reminiscent of words Jesus spoke to His disciples the night before He died. He said, "You will be witnesses because you are the ones with Me from the beginning" (John 15:27).

What Our Involvement Isn't

With this background, perhaps we can more readily recognize that we cannot be witnesses to Jesus in the same sense as the earliest New Testament Christians. In fact, even St. Paul was not an *eyewitness* to Jesus' three-year career in Judea and Galilee. In his first sermon recorded in Acts, Paul said, "*We* preach the Good News to you," but he added that others were the witnesses who saw Jesus alive for many days after His resurrection (13:31–32). Of course, Paul did have first-hand contact with the risen Christ on the road to Damascus, as well as at other times. On the road, Paul was appointed to be a witness to the things he had seen about Jesus and to the things that Jesus would show him from that time on (26:16; see 22:15).

We cannot be witnesses in the same sense used in Acts. But in the strongest possible way, I want to encourage Christians to tell the Good News. In fact, I have set for myself a daring goal to speak about Jesus Christ to at least one person every day. Often this occurs on the airplane as I converse with the occupant of the next seat. Especially at those times, it helps me to remember who I am and what I am doing.

I am not an *eyewitness* to the first-century career of Christ as He walked on the earth. I did not see Him alive after He died. If anything, the things that I have seen with my eyes add up to bad news, not good. I have seen disease, sadness, and tears. I have witnessed crime, cruelty, and despair. Through television I have seen wars and unspeakable atrocities. In short, I am a witness to a world of sin. And I have seen people die. While I have seen happy things too, the pall of death looms over them all. That's the way it is in a sinful world. The wage paid by sin is, indeed, death.

If I'm going to offer truly good news to the person in the seat next to mine, it can't come from what my senses have experienced. And it surely can't come from any old thing that comes to my mind to say. Instead, I speak the Good News as I point to Jesus Christ through the witness made by those who accompanied Him, saw Him alive, and spoke with Him after His death on the cross and His resurrection.

The Good News I have to share is that in Jesus Christ, God became man to pay the price for all human sin, including yours and mine. Then He rose from the dead and gave us life. If you or I had been among those who saw Him at the time, there would have been nothing we could do to add to or to improve on this great work. We could only bear witness to it. Peter said:

> We are witnesses of all the things He did in the country of the Jews and in Jerusalem. They hanged Him on a cross and killed Him. God raised Him on the third day and revealed Him—not to all the people but to us, the witnesses chosen by God who ate and drank with Him after He rose from the dead. *(10:39–41)*

For our part, we certainly can't add to the saving work of Christ. We can only speak about it to others, recognizing that this remains the most important thing in the world.

The fact that Jesus Christ died is more important than the fact that *I* shall die, and the fact that Jesus Christ rose from the dead is the sole ground of my hope that I, too, shall be raised on the Last Day. Our salvation is "external to ourselves." I find no salvation in my life history, but only in the history of Jesus Christ. *(LT, p. 54, emphasis original)*

What Our Involvement Is

It is into the death and resurrection of Christ that we are baptized, passing through death into life with Him (Romans 6:1–11). It is the body and blood with which He made the one-and-only sacrifice for sin that He gives us to eat and drink in His Supper. In these sacraments, as through the Gospel, the most important thing in all the world becomes ours. We are among those who have not seen and yet have believed by the power of God (John 20:29; 1 John 5:6–10).

It is in this sense that we can be used by the Lord today to help bring the blessings of Christ's work to others. This is what happens when we speak the Gospel to them, putting them in contact with the central message of the Scriptures.

In His High Priestly Prayer, Jesus said, "I do not pray for these [the apostles] only, but also concerning *those who will believe in Me* through their word [that is, through the word of the apostles]" (John 17:20, emphasis added). That's us and those to whom we speak the Gospel based on Scripture! When we tell others about Christ, the spotlight comes off us, our experiences, and our ideas—even off the ancient witnesses such as Peter or Paul. Instead, it falls squarely on Jesus.

No, we are not witnesses in the sense of Acts 1:8. But that's okay. We aren't in Jerusalem either, nor in Judea or Samaria. That's okay too. We are at the "ends of the earth" on the geographical outline of Acts 1:8. And here, no less than in the first century, the Holy Spirit witnesses to Christ as we share the Gospel with others (Acts 5:32; see John 14:26; 15:26; 16:8–11, 13–15). This is what we mean when we talk about witnessing to Christ today.

Our concern, then, is to get the Word out. We need to speak it to family and friends, to acquaintances, and to people with whom we come into contact only once. As we share this Good News with others—as we sow the seed of the Gospel—the Holy Spirit will bless it. He really will.

On with the task, then, of sharing the message of Christ with others. And God bless as you do.

Chapter 5

The Shape of Church Life

Read Acts 2:42–7:60

We've moved rather deliberately thus far on our

trip through Acts. If we were traveling by train, you could say we have been pulling away from the station rather slowly! This pace is beneficial, though, because we have encountered many significant details in Acts 1 and 2 that require close observation. But in this chapter, with our previous studies having laid the tracks for our journey, a clear railway lies ahead. Now we will move more rapidly. Please note that you will need to read a relatively large portion of Acts along with this chapter.

Skimming

You may be tempted to skim through this lengthy reading assignment in Acts. If you find skimming necessary, that's all right. While it would be good to read this portion of Acts with the same close attention to detail we have used with previous shorter sections, it's okay to skim God's Word.

Skimming is especially good if you are trying to pick up the general drift without getting too involved in the details. Later you can return to cover the same ground more carefully, especially once you have the "lay of the land." I often skim the Scriptures. Frequently it opens portals that take me further into the inspired text.

The Shape of the Early Church

As we *pay attention to internal organization,* Acts 2:42–7:60 gives us a glimpse of the early church at the first stage of the geographic outline found in Acts 1:8. This large portion of Acts covers the church's life in

Jerusalem during the days following the momentous Pentecost described in Acts 2. Luke writes that "they were continuing in the teaching of the apostles and in fellowship, in the breaking of bread and in the prayers" (2:42). Together, these four elements make up the shape of the first-century Christians' life together in the Lord.

To these early Christians, the "apostles' teaching"—whether delivered at the divine service or openly to all in the temple (3:12–4:2) or before the Sanhedrin (the Jewish Council, see 4:8–12; 5:29–32)—was neither a bore nor a chore. Instead, they knew this doctrine or teaching brought the reality of their salvation in the Lord Jesus Christ to them with all the power of God.

Their fellowship was sharing together in the same faith of the heart and the same confession of the lips (see Romans 10:9; 1 Corinthians 1:10). It also showed itself in acts of genuine love and concern for one another (4:32–37; 5:12–16; 6:1–6).

The "breaking of bread" has been understood by numerous scholars to mean the Lord's Supper. While I have always aligned myself with that group, I also admit that a similar phrase in Acts 2:46 seems to refer to the everyday meals Christians ate in great joy and humility. In either case, we can learn a lesson. Whether we are receiving the forgiveness of our sins in the Lord's Supper or living the forgiven life with those closest to us, we are God's people.

We also learn from the perseverance in prayer the early Christians demonstrated. Undoubtedly they prayed as they gathered for worship. We also find that they went to the temple at appointed hours (3:1) and prayed at unscheduled times in response to specific needs and challenges that surfaced (4:24–30).

The Shape of the Modern Church

Our circumstances of time and place differ markedly from those of the early Christians living in Jerusalem. But we can see in this portion of Acts the same general, ongoing shape of life together in the Lord that should characterize His church in every age, including ours.

We hear a great deal today about "Jesus and me" spirituality. Those who subscribe to this philosophy tend to lose sight of the church for their focus on the individual. I find it refreshing to be reminded that, from its beginning in Acts, the Christian church has been just that, a *church*—people called and gathered around the Word. It began that way at Pentecost and remained that way in the weeks, months, and centuries thereafter.

"In this Christian community," the *Large Catechism* says, "we have forgiveness of sins, which is given to us through the holy sacraments and absolution as well as through all the comforting passages of the entire Gospel" (Janzow, p. 75; LC II 54). May our Father in heaven grant this to us all our days. Hallowed be His name; His kingdom come!

Proclaimers with a Proclamation

In the church, God has given us not only a Gospel to proclaim, but also official proclaimers to speak it (Ephesians 4:11; Romans 10:14–15). Unfortunately, many people think the church's life during its earliest days did not include a distinct office of the ministry. Some argue that this office emerged later. Scholars and others have speculated that in the bubbly and exciting times described in the initial part of Acts, the church would have accepted those Christians with the most evident "charisma," however defined, as best able to provide "leadership." In this scenario, there would have been little or no attention given to official position.

Two important biblical observations will help us evaluate this claim. First, as members of a minority in Jerusalem surrounded by many people who did not believe in Jesus as Savior, individual Christians surely would have had many opportunities to speak of their faith with unbelievers, whether one on one or in groups. This was the case, Martin Luther wrote, with Stephen and Philip. These two men were among the seven deacons appointed in Acts 6 to serve tables. But Luther observed that Stephen did more than take care of food distribution. He also "wrought signs and wonders among the people, disputed with members of the synagogue and refuted the council of the Jews with the word of the Spirit [Acts 6:8]" (LW, vol. 40, p. 38).

Luther asked what right and authority Stephen had to do such things. He answered this question in the instance of Stephen and also of Philip: "They did it on their own initiative ... since the door was open to them, and they saw the need of a people who were ignorant and deprived of the Word." Luther also wrote, "In the same way any Christian should feel obligated to act" (LW, vol. 40, p. 38).

The second biblical observation more directly addresses the claim that a distinct office of the ministry did not exist in the early church. Simply put, Acts says otherwise, even at this budding stage of the church's life.

In the last chapter, we saw that even those who had been taught by Jesus Himself, before and after the resurrection, still received His authorization to take the Gospel to the ends of the earth (1:8; contrast Jeremiah 23:21, 32). Further, we noted the requirements set forth for the man who would replace Judas. The pool of candidates for this position consisted only of males (1:20–22). Now in Acts 6:2, we find that the seven deacons were appointed, first, because it was not right for the apostles to neglect their preaching and teaching responsibilities with respect to God's Word. This means there was an office of the ministry dating back to the earliest days of the church. Originally the apostles exercised this office, which had its own authorization and qualifications. This office also had limits as to who could and could not serve in it. And the office of the ministry was given an overarching responsibility that shaped the day-to-day decisions of those who held it.

Of course, today there are no eyewitnesses of Christ's career. Consequently, there are no apostles anymore. But the same commission the apostles had—to preach the Gospel and forgive sins—continues. It is the commission to shepherd the sheep, if you will. Now it is carried out by pastors. The German translation of the *Treatise on the Power and Primacy of the Pope,* one of the Lutheran Confessions, notes that the office of the ministry "proceeds from the common call of the apostles" (par. 10).

This fact remains true whether we are discussing pastors in the first century or in the late 20th century (see 20:28; 1 Peter 5:1–4; 2 Timothy 2:2). The shape of the church's life still includes an office of the ministry, by God's command and institution, whose members publicly deliver the Gospel and sacraments to people.

As this office of the ministry is carried forward by faithful pastors, we can thank God not only for the pastoral office He has instituted, but also for the men who faithfully serve in this capacity. What a great gift to the church.

Persecution

One major emphasis stands out in Acts 2:42–7:60. It can't be ignored, even if we just skim the text. It is the cold, hard reality of persecution.

The early church felt persecution acutely. For example, through Peter and John, the Lord worked a miraculous healing for a lame man. But because they proclaimed the risen Christ, the Jewish officials did not thank them. Instead, the officials interrogated and threatened Peter and John. The same people who had not long before tried Jesus were now persecuting His followers (4:1–22). Later, the apostles were thrown in jail, threatened again, and finally beaten prior to their release (5:17–40). Things were going from bad to worse.

Acts mentions that the church initially enjoyed favor from the populace (2:47; 4:21; 5:13, 26). But the more fierce the persecution became, the less mention Acts makes of favorable responses to Christians from the people of Jerusalem. At this stage of church history, the climactic episode of persecution was Stephen's stoning by an enraged Sanhedrin (7:51–60). Persecution threatened to knock the infant church out of shape or even out of existence.

Amid all this trouble, the power of the Holy Spirit rose to the occasion. The same apostles who ran and scattered when Jesus was arrested in the Garden of Gethsemane now boldly proclaimed their Lord, even in the presence of those who had handed Him over to the Romans to be killed. They stated to all that "there is salvation in no one else like Him, nor is there any other name under heaven which has been and still is given among men by which we must be saved" (4:12). When the council repeated its order to shut up about Jesus, Peter and the apostles answered, "It is necessary for us to obey God rather than men" (5:29).

The initial persecution of the church in Jerusalem is noteworthy not only for what the apostles said to the authorities, but also for what the church said to her Lord. This too is part of the shape of church life in this world. Recognizing the guiding and protecting hand of the Lord, the church prayed for added boldness (4:24–30). There was rejoicing because they had been counted worthy to suffer dishonor for the name of Jesus (5:41). The persecuted church grew stronger in the Lord.

Sometimes we act as if the church grows best when it presents its most attractive face and blends, however it can, into its surroundings. During the church's early days, though, the apostles and members, including Stephen, clearly demarcated the difference between Christianity and the surrounding religions. They were treated harshly as a result. But the church was in better shape than anyone could have guessed. In fact, it grew—both in numbers (2:47; 4:4; 5:14; 6:7) and in spiritual maturity.

We may not experience persecution like that described in Acts 2:42–7:60. But in bad days as well as in good, our task is to continue to stand tall for the Lord. We know that the same God who protected and blessed the early Christians during persecution and turmoil is with us in our lives and work.

The church always needs to be what she is in the Lord Jesus Christ. He shapes the church's life day after day so even when faced with trouble and persecution, she remains "the mother that brings forth and bears every Christian through the Word of God" (Janzow, p. 73; LC II 42). Thanks be to God for this great assurance in Jesus Christ.

Chapter 6

The Big Target

Read Acts 8

It is easy to major in minors, missing the big targets in life because we never get around to taking aim at them. Instead, we become preoccupied with a variety of lesser targets, lesser goals. In many cases, these lesser things may not be bad. In fact, we get caught up in them partly because they are good. Still, they keep us from the highest, most important priorities.

Thus far, the story in Acts of the young Christian church has been impressive and exciting. We already have read that even "a great crowd of the priests became obedient to the faith" (6:7). However, that same verse indicates that it was the number of disciples in Jerusalem that had increased greatly. The Gospel of Christ was supposed to go out far and wide, but here, about a quarter of the way through Acts, we still find ourselves in Jerusalem.

Moving Out

The Lord indeed works in strange ways. Just as we begin to wonder how the Good News will spread, we read about the "great persecution" (8:1). In large numbers, Christians left the holy city for the countryside of Judea and Samaria. The Christians scattered, but they spread the Good News as they went (8:4). The Lord was pushing the church toward the Gentile world—nudging it along the lines of the Master's statement about the geographic expansion of Christianity.

In Acts 8, as a result of horrible and violent persecution, the Gospel reached the second theater of missionary activity Jesus mentioned in Acts 1:8—Judea and Samaria. As we *pay attention to internal organization,* we realize that even if the early Christians' mission vision had not grown to worldwide proportions yet, the Lord was moving it in that direction.

Samaria

As the Christians moved out from Jerusalem, one of the first areas they entered was Samaria. In its unique way, this step constituted a huge leap forward. Readers of the gospels will recall that bad blood existed between Jews and Samaritans. For example, we find real animosity expressed in accounts such as that of Jesus and the Samaritan woman at the well (John 4:5–42). The gospel according to St. Luke mentions the Samaritans in several telling passages: when Jesus wanted to travel through Samaria (Luke 9:51–55); the Samaritan leper who thanked Jesus for healing him (Luke 17:11–19); and Jesus' story of the Good Samaritan (Luke 10:25–37).

It is not difficult to imagine that the beleaguered young church may have had doubts about whether it was moving in the right direction, especially if the road seemed to be leading into Samaria. So the Lord gave His church some encouraging pats on the back (see Acts 8).

Receiving the Holy Spirit

First, the Lord encouraged the church through Philip's experience with the Samaritans. He proclaimed Christ to them (8:5), baptized them (8:12), and they found great joy in everything (8:8). They believed the message Philip brought them (8:12).

But Acts says that the Holy Spirit had not fallen on them. Instead, they only had been baptized into the name of the Lord Jesus (8:16). This is an amazing statement in light of Peter's statement on Pentecost: "Repent and be baptized, each of you, in the name of Jesus Christ for the forgiveness of your sins, and you will receive the gift of the Holy Spirit" (2:38).

These two Bible passages might seem to contradict each other. In Acts 2:38, the Bible says that those who are baptized receive the Holy Spirit while in Acts 8:16, it reports an instance of baptism in which the Holy Spirit was not received. Acts 8:16 does note that the Holy Spirit had *"not yet* fallen on any of them" (emphasis added), but we cannot solve this problem by merely recognizing a delay in the fulfillment of the Acts 2:38 promise. Like everyone else, the Samaritans needed the Spirit to believe in the first place because "no one can say 'Jesus is Lord' except by the Holy Spirit" (1 Corinthians 12:3).

God does not contradict Himself. Here, as in other cases, understanding exactly what the passages are talking about is vital. Are these passages really talking about the same thing?

If we examine Acts 8 more closely, we discover several clues. First, it says the Samaritans eventually received the Holy Spirit, but only after Peter and John arrived from Jerusalem and laid hands on them (8:14–17). Second, this outpouring of the Holy Spirit must have happened in some outward way because a man named Simon could tell that it had occurred. He even offered Peter money so he too could lay hands on people and have them receive the Spirit (8:18–24).

We can see that the reception of the Holy Spirit mentioned in Acts 8, the one that did *not* happen immediately upon the Samaritans' baptism, must have stood out as an extraordinary manifestation of divine power. God seems to have provided it (at least in part) for the benefit of Peter and John as the representatives of the Jerusalem church and the other apostles. It was delayed until they arrived. Only then did the Lord pour out His Holy Spirit in a way that could be observed.

Can you imagine what a tremendous encouragement this became for the church? Peter and John could return to Jerusalem and say, "It's okay to reach out to the Samaritans. This is the right move." The Lord was gently pushing the church further and further toward the Gentiles, moving it toward the big target of outreach to the ends of the earth.

On their way back to Jerusalem, Peter and John showed that they got the point. They brought the saving Gospel to Samaritan villages (8:25). What a moment for John, who once had wanted to call down fire from heaven on a Samaritan village (Luke 9:54)!

The public manifestation of the Spirit's work mentioned in Acts 8:17 seems not to have been the same thing that Peter meant when he said on Pentecost that the great blessings of baptism are the forgiveness of sins and the gift of the Holy Spirit (2:38). Even before Peter and John arrived from Jerusalem, the Samaritans already believed and rejoiced in the Gospel. They had the Holy Spirit, otherwise there would have been no believing and rejoicing. "That which is born of the flesh is flesh," Jesus had said, "but that which is born of the Spirit is spirit" (John 3:6; Romans 15:13).

The Acts 2:38 promise had come true indeed

among the Samaritans. At their baptism, they *did* receive the Holy Spirit—exactly as Peter had meant at Pentecost. But no one knew this simply by looking at them. On the other hand, the reception of the Holy Spirit that occurred later in Acts 8 was an outward confirmation from the Lord that the church was on the right track, moving toward the whole world.

The extraordinary coming of the Spirit also told the Samaritans something. It showed them that salvation truly was from the Jews, as Jesus had told the Samaritan woman at the well (John 4:22). The Messiah had come from the Jews. His chosen apostles were Jews. When the newly converted Samaritans received this outward manifestation of the Spirit, they could conclude that they needed to change their thinking. No longer should they look at Jews like Peter and John and the Jerusalem Christians with their old attitude of disdain (see Luke 9:53). They all had received the same Spirit, and they all were members of the same church (1 Corinthians 12:13; Ephesians 4:3–6).

Acts 8 does not say exactly how people realized the Samaritans had received the Holy Spirit. Elsewhere in Acts, the outpouring of the Holy Spirit was marked by speaking in tongues (2:4, 11; 10:46–47; 19:6). In Acts 2, this meant speaking in established human languages previously unknown to the speaker. If the Acts 8 manifestation of the Spirit included speaking in tongues, it is not at all unrealistic to see this as the same phenomenon we find in Acts 2. Simon the magician might have thought he had found something he could capitalize on. The prospect of offering instant language-learning to people would have caught his attention.

The Lord gave His church several "pats on the back" as it took its first tentative steps toward worldwide mission. It's important that we observe these events as we read in Acts about the remarkable manifestations of the Holy Spirit. Acts does not promise that other Christians would receive these manifestations, nor does the rest of Scripture make such promises. However, there might be an unwarranted tendency for sincere Christians today to think there is something wrong with their faith if they do not undergo remarkable outpourings of the Spirit. It helps me to remember that the Lord used manifestations like those in Acts 8 to encourage the church in its mission to non-Jews—Samaritans, in this case. Acts depicts an unusual situation in which outward outpourings of the Holy Spirit occurred—a set of circumstances that has not existed as such since the first century.

The Good News of the Suffering Servant

I find it interesting that the last part of Acts 8 (vv. 26–40) tells the story of Philip and the Ethiopian eunuch. Here again we find the Lord giving His church a "pat on the back" and broadening its mission horizon. The Spirit told Philip to join this foreigner in his chariot. It turns out the Ethiopian was reading the magnificent words of Isaiah 53 about the Suffering Servant who did not open His mouth and was sacrificed for the sins of the people. When the

Ethiopian asked whom the prophet was speaking about, Philip seized the opportunity to open his mouth (8:35) and told the Ethiopian the Good News of prophecy fulfilled, payment made, and sins forgiven in Jesus Christ.

You know the result: A convert to Christ was headed to his homeland with the Good News. The target of mission to the Gentiles was getting bigger and bigger in the sights. In the next two chapters, we will move into Acts 9–11 and see how the Lord took His people a couple major strides closer to the big target.

The Lord has given us the same Good News to share with others. Perhaps it is someone you have worked with for years and yet have never spoken to about the Lord. Maybe it is a neighbor, someone with whom you have discussed flowers, sporting events, children, or grandchildren, but not Christ. Or perhaps your big target is someone in your household. Evangelism targets are out there, and they are very real.

Let's not forget to shoot at the big target when sharing the Good News with those around us and with the whole world. As we do, God will pour out His blessings to the ends of the earth.

Section C

Pay Attention to What Is Repeated

I will never forget our family vacation in the summer of 1969. We packed the Winnebago and headed for the West Coast—a much longer trip than we usually took. As we journeyed over the plains and across the Rocky Mountains toward California, each day brought something new to see, some exciting new experience.

At times the excitement was more than we bargained for, especially for me. After a few days in sunny California, we turned east and headed back to the Midwest. Our travel plans took us over the Tioga Pass. What beautiful scenery! Gradually we approached the summit and started down the eastern slope of the pass. One road sign after another advised drivers pulling trailers to shift to a lower gear to avoid brake problems. We must have passed at least five such signs, but the grade looked so gradual that I decided to remain in high gear, despite the repeated warnings.

You guessed it. Before long, I smelled something strange. My brakes were overheating. Now I was faced with the problem of stopping our fully loaded car and trailer. An alert driver sensed my problem and rendered some much-needed assistance by pulling in front of us and letting us bump into the back of his car to help us slow down.

Without a doubt, this event reinforced the importance of *paying attention to what is repeated.* After all, what is repeated is usually important!

In Acts, we repeatedly encounter two events. In fact, each event stands out as so significant that it comes up three different times. With each event, the story is told, repeated, and repeated again.

One repeated story is the conversion of Paul. We have the account in Acts 9. Then Paul tells it in Acts 22 and in Acts 26. The other repeated story is the conversion of the household of Cornelius. The account is in Acts 10, but Peter repeats it in Acts 11 and in Acts 15. These two incidents, told and retold, give us vital clues to the message of Acts. In the next two chapters, we will examine these events closely.

Chapter 7

Faithfulness and Outreach Part I

Read Acts 9:1–31; 22:1–22; 26:1–32

In this chapter, we will devote our attention to the first of the two events that are repeated in Acts—the conversion of Paul. Like the story of Peter and Cornelius, which we will cover in the next chapter, Paul's conversion stood out as an important milestone in the developing mission to the Gentile world.

Mission to the Gentiles

At the beginning of Acts 9, we find Saul of Tarsus on his way to round up Christians and jail them, or even worse. This was the same man who had held the garments of those who had stoned Stephen. Saul agreed totally with that act (7:58; 8:1) and had made something of a name for himself as a persecutor of the early Christian church (8:3). This time Saul was headed to the city of Damascus. On this day, though, it would be no routine run.

On the way, Saul saw Jesus. The Lord asked, "Saul, Saul, why are you persecuting Me?" (9:4). This was an important moment in the history of the church. Although he did not know it at the time, this man Saul (later called Paul) was going to be the apostle to the Gentiles. That was what the Lord wanted him to be. Already when He surprised Ananias with the instruction to baptize the persecutor Saul, Christ said, "This one is My chosen vessel to carry My name before the nations." Jesus was announcing that Paul would preach the Gospel to the Gentiles (Acts 9:15; see Galatians 1:15–16).

Many have pointed out, and rightly so, that Paul was the 13th apostle. So far the early church had taken pains to keep it at 12. After Judas killed himself, the lot fell on Matthias (1:23–26) to bring the number back to 12. Jesus had chosen 12 apostles, just as there had been 12 tribes in Israel, each descended from one of the 12 sons of Jacob. But in the New Testament era, the Good News would go out far and wide. It was going to spill beyond the borders of Israel, so there were not 12 apostles anymore, but 13!

Later Paul recalled that shortly after his conversion, the Lord appeared to him and said, "Go, I will send you far off to the Gentiles" (Acts 22:21). Paul recounted this as he faced an angry mob near the temple in Jerusalem. In a way, repeating Christ's words was the wrong thing to say to that group. It caused them to riot. In another way, though, it was exactly the right thing to do. Obviously, Jesus' words had made a huge impression on Paul. When he wrote to the Ephesians, who were mostly Gentiles, Paul said, "But now in Christ Jesus, you who were *far off* have been brought near in the blood of Christ" (Ephesians 2:13, emphasis added). Indeed they had been brought near because someone like Paul took God's Word to them.

It was God's plan that Paul would be the apostle to the Gentiles. By the grace of God, this was a mission that Paul would throw himself into with great vigor. He had agreed with the "pillars of the church" in Jerusalem—James, Peter, and John—that he and his associates would go out to the Gentile world (Galatians 2:9). He wrote to the Romans: "I am the apostle to the Gentiles and I magnify my ministry" (Romans 11:13). The same Paul who once had been so eager to go to faraway cities to track down and persecute Christians was now anxious to go to faraway cities in the service of his Lord to proclaim the Gospel. The conversion of Paul had "mission to the Gentiles" written all over it. But that isn't all.

Justification by Grace for Christ's Sake through Faith

There is a second element to the conversion of Paul. It is really the other side of the coin of mission to the Gentiles. Paul's conversion also had written all over it the central truth of the Christian faith: justification by grace for Christ's sake through faith.

With this point, we move onto some familiar ground, but I suspect this wonderful teaching lies so squarely beneath our noses that we don't see it. We act surprised when we see justification by grace emerge from Scripture in another place, especially if this is a place we didn't expect to find it. But this message is here in the account of Paul's conversion. In fact, when we stop to think about it, justification by grace is the only way to explain why a man like Saul of Tarsus could be welcomed into the church of Jesus Christ. Much later in Acts (and in his epistles), Paul reported how zealous he had been for the traditions of his ancestors and about how good a Pharisee he had tried to be. He described his previous life to the Philippians by saying he was

> circumcised on the eighth day, of the nation of Israel, of the tribe of Benjamin, a Hebrew of the Hebrews, as to the law a Pharisee, as to zeal a persecutor of the church, as to righteousness which comes about in the law blameless. But the various things in which I was coming out ahead, I came to think of as one great big loss on account of Christ. Indeed, I go on considering them as a loss because of what surpasses them, the knowledge of Christ Jesus my Lord. On account of Him I have lost all things. I regard them as repugnant rubbish in order that I might gain Christ and be found in Him, not having my own righteousness which proceeds from the law but righteousness through faith in Christ—the kind that comes from God by faith. *(Philippians 3:5–9)*

Paul was saying that the robe of righteousness that Christ had prepared for him, that Christ placed on him, that he received by faith, was better than any robe of righteousness he could have fashioned himself. No matter how zealous he was, how faithful or how sincere according to the traditions of his ancestors, Paul always would fall short of God's holy demands.

In 1 Timothy, Paul said that he had been "a blasphemer, a persecutor, and an insolent person." He added that "the grace of our God overflowed with faith and love that are in Christ Jesus. The saying is faithful and worthy of whole-hearted acceptance: Christ Jesus came into the world to save sinners, of whom I am number one" (1 Timothy 1:13–15).

We immediately recognize that every one of us can say those words. This is what justification by grace for Christ's sake through faith means in our lives. On account of Paul and in his place, Jesus cried on the cross, "My God, My God, why have You forsaken Me?" (Matthew 27:46). And on account of you and me too. On account of Paul—the blasphemer, the persecutor, the murderer—Jesus said, "It is finished" (John 19:30) and died. And on account of you and me too.

Faithfulness and Outreach

The conversion of Paul emphasizes mission to the Gentiles *and* justification by grace for Christ's sake through faith. We must be concerned about outreach to the world that springs from a faithful reception of the Gospel in our hearts. *Faithfulness* and *outreach* are two key words. To say it another way, "Keep the message straight! Get the message out!" It's comforting to find this dual message in Acts repeated each time the story of Paul's conversion is discussed.

The Centrality of Justification

We can rejoice at the repetition of the message of faithfulness and outreach, especially regarding the teaching of justification. It's so easy to lose track of this gift. Before we know it, we find ourselves thinking everything would be too simple—too easy—because our justification doesn't come from ourselves. But there was nothing easy about our justification from Christ's point of view. What comes as a free gift to us was bought at the price of His blood shed for us.

The truth of justification by God's grace becomes the foundation for our faithfulness to God. Martin Luther, who knew a thing or two about justification, put it this way: "Where this single article remains pure, Christendom will remain pure, in beautiful harmony, and without any schisms. But where it does not remain pure, it is impossible to repel any error or heretical spirit" (Tappert, p. 540; FC SD III 6).

Justification by faith is not *justification by our faithfulness.* God does not check to see how faithful we are and then decide whether He will justify us. When we realize how the reality of justification reaches out and gives people God's riches at Christ's expense, then everything fits together. Instead of *our* pride insisting on getting the things *we* want, when and where *we* want them, we receive God's gifts as *He* gives them. And we rejoice that He is the one doing the giving and we are the ones doing the receiving.

Over the years, I have declared to many people, in sermons and in private conversations, this tremendous truth of Holy Scripture. As I have done so, I have sensed the same joy and reassurance that I find in this forgiving message from our God. We never can hear it too often. Likewise, we never can thank God enough for it. As we do, we can join with Paul and millions of others through the centuries in saying, "Praise God, it is true. Praise God, it is true."

Chapter 8

Faithfulness and Outreach Part II

Read Acts 10:1–11:16; 15:7–11

In the last chapter we applied the principle *pay attention to what is repeated* as we read portions of Acts. We observed that there are two events of such importance that each is repeated three times in Acts—the conversion of Paul and Peter's visit to the home of Cornelius. Peter's visit to Cornelius will occupy us in this chapter.

We already have observed that the conversion of Paul points to mission to the Gentiles and to justification by grace for Christ's sake through faith. So does the story of Peter and Cornelius.

Mission to the Gentiles

Cornelius was a Roman, an officer in the army. He was not a Jew nor was his family. They were Gentiles, Romans—God-fearing ones but Romans all the same (10:1–2). They were not religiously mixed-up distant cousins of the Jews like the Samaritans. They probably were not proselytes—people who had come into Judaism as adult converts—so the males would not have been circumcised.

Many things could have tempted Peter to say no when the opportunity arose for him to visit the home of this Roman centurion. He could have experienced ethnic prejudice, the kind of thing that moves folks to say, "Do we have to let *those* people in? And if we let them in, what problems will we have? Will we be filled with suspicion or maybe even jealous that they're here?" As time went by and the Gentiles started to enter the church, such problems did arise. Before too long, in fact, Gentile Christians outnumbered Jewish Christians. But this wasn't an excuse to avoid reaching out to Gentiles, people who had been bought with the blood of Christ.

But mission to the Gentiles wasn't an easy step to take. Cornelius' messengers found Peter at the seacoast city of Joppa. From that same city centuries before, another messenger of the Lord Most High, a prophet named Jonah, had boarded a ship and sailed into the Mediterranean because he didn't want to go to the Gentiles (Jonah 1:3ff). Now there was Peter, a messenger of the Lord God, and the question presented itself again. Would he also try to turn tail and run? He would not, partly because the Lord had prepared him ahead of time with a vision.

In the vision, Peter saw a big sheet coming down from heaven. It opened up and there were all sorts of animals deemed unclean according to ceremonial law—the kind of thing Peter ordinarily would have nothing to do with. But the voice of God said, "Rise, Peter, kill and eat" (10:10–13). Just in case Peter had any lingering doubts, he discovered upon his arrival at Cornelius' home that Cornelius had experienced a vision in which an angel told him to send his men to Joppa to get Peter (10:30–33, which retells 10:3–8). Sure enough, the messengers had knocked on the door just after Peter's vision had ended (10:17–18).

Peter preached to Cornelius' household, Gentiles all, and the Holy Spirit was poured out on them in the same way He had been poured out on Pentecost. Peter said, "The Holy Spirit fell on them, just as also upon us, at the beginning" (11:15). Again, Peter said, "God gave the same gift to them as to us" (11:17). Remember, the prophecy that Peter quoted on Pentecost had said that God would pour out His Spirit on *all* flesh (2:17). With the baptism of Cornelius' household (10:47–48), the door to take the Gospel to the ends of the earth (1:8) was standing wide open before the church.

Justification by Grace for Christ's Sake through Faith

Not only is the story of Peter and Cornelius about mission to the Gentiles, it is also about justification by grace for Christ's sake through faith. This emphasis on justification began already in Peter's vision. The sheet unfurled to reveal the ceremonially unclean animals and the voice said, "Kill and eat." Peter answered, "Lord, they're unclean." The voice responded, "What God calls clean, don't go calling unclean" (10:13–15).

This refers back to Christ Himself. He said it is not the things that go into a person that defile him, but the things that come out. The gospel according to St. Mark

75

states that when Jesus said this, He was declaring all foods clean (Mark 7:14–23). Jesus would pay for saying things like that, not only because people would grow angry at Him for making such statements and kill Him, but also because this was what God wanted. Jesus was going to the cross not because *people* put Him there, but because *God* made Him the great sacrifice. He was the only one able to pay for the sins of the whole world down to this very day—yours and mine too. No mere man could do it, but this was the man who was also God.

Justification by grace also is taught as the story of Peter and Cornelius reaches its climax—the pouring out of the Holy Spirit on people who had lived their entire lives without the Old Testament law. If salvation really were by the law, these people never should have received the Holy Spirit. Because they did receive the Holy Spirit, it is evident that salvation is not by works of the law. As Peter told them, "About Him [Jesus] all the prophets testify that everyone who believes in Him receives forgiveness of sins through His name" (10:43).

Through this incident, Peter came to a greater appreciation of the grace of God. He did not fail to notice that the Holy Spirit descended on his audience while he was still speaking to them. Here the answer was vividly given to the question that Paul would pose later in one of his epistles: "Did you receive the Spirit by the works of the law or by hearing with faith?" (Galatians 3:2). The Gentiles in Cornelius' family obviously did not receive the Spirit by the works of the law. They received Him by hearing with faith.

This realization was so burned into Peter's memory that later, at the apostolic council in Jerusalem, he recalled what happened with Cornelius and his family. Peter said, "Why do you put God to the test, placing a burden on the neck of the [Gentile] disciples which neither our fathers nor we ourselves could bear? We believe that we will be saved through the grace of the Lord Jesus, the same way they will" (15:10–11).

The Mission Today

Sometimes we say, "If only we were more like the saints of the first-century church, back in the heroic days." But we are a lot like them. We also say, "Do we have to let *those* people in?" For example, would our congregations readily accept people of a lower economic status than most members enjoy? Would we find it difficult to treat people we know have past histories of drunk driving or burglary as brothers and sisters in Christ? Can we give a genuine, heartfelt welcome to those whom "polite society" has shunned?

Let's be more pointed and honest with ourselves. Not only in our congregations as a whole but also in our individual hearts and minds, don't we find ourselves asking, "Do we have to let *those* people in?" We believe that God loved the world, but do we really find it easy to think that He loved certain "undesirables"? Do we act as though we believe that He wants us to share our love and care with them as well as the blessings of salvation?

It's a good thing the message about mission to the Gentiles is repeated in Acts. After all, pep talks will not fuel the kind of outreach that has been going on in the church for centuries. Instead, there is something about the Gospel message itself that simply will not stay contained. It reaches out to the ends of the earth, touching people where they are and drawing them in.

As we have seen, the other side of the coin of mission to the Gentiles is justification by grace for Christ's sake through faith. This is the key! Justification by grace forms our power and impetus for outreach. This Good News reaches out to people just as they are—dead in trespasses and sins, without hope and without God in the world (Ephesians 2:1, 12). It draws them in by showering on them all the blessings of Christ's life, death, and resurrection.

Justification by grace for Christ's sake through faith also reminds Christians that it is the Lord who owns the church, not we. He purchased it at the high cost of sacrificing Himself, and He imposes no restrictions or qualifications of birth or behavior for entry into His church. Indeed, the blessed reality of justification and mission to the Gentiles do go together.

Two Sides of the Same Coin

As we examine how Acts describes the conversion of Paul and the incident of Peter and Cornelius, we find justification by grace and mission to the Gentiles mentioned side by side. In the last account in Acts of Paul's conversion, Paul said God sent him to the Gentiles "*to open their eyes* that they may turn from darkness to light and from the authority of Satan to God, that they may *receive forgiveness of sins* and a share among those who are sanctified *by faith*" (26:18, emphasis added). After Peter reported the conversion of Cornelius' family, the Jerusalem church glorified God and said, "God has also *given* the *Gentiles* repentance unto life" (Acts 11:18, emphasis added).

Martin Luther also noticed this prominence of both justification by grace and mission to the Gentiles. He observed that Acts "emphasizes so powerfully not only the preaching of the apostles about faith in Christ … but also the examples and the instances of this teaching, how the Gentiles as well as Jews were justified through the Gospel alone, without the law" (LW vol. 35, 363). Elsewhere he said, "Therefore, in … Acts, taken as a whole, nothing is discussed except that Jews as well as Gentiles, righteous men as well as sinners, are to be justified solely by faith in Christ Jesus, without Law or works" (LW vol. 26, 205).

In the last chapter, we looked at two key ideas—*faithfulness* and *outreach*. These are the key ideas we find repeated and underlined in Acts. *Faithfulness* and *outreach* matter not because I say so, but because they arise from Scripture. They are vital to the life of the church. Mission to the Gentiles speaks of *outreach*. And justification by grace for Christ's sake through faith has to remain the cornerstone of all our *faithfulness* to God's Word.

As I write these words, I reflect on news of the passing of a middle-aged pastor I had come to know over the past three years. His ministry clearly identified two hallmarks in his pastoral life. First, he knew the power of that glorious message about justification by grace for Christ's sake through faith. How clearly he believed, declared, and lived that truth of his confession! I also saw in his ministry a strong desire to reach out to people with the message of salvation. Marked by these two characteristics, his ministry was a real blessing to those he served. I could only pray, "God, continue to bless us with this kind of pastor and this kind of laity. Please, God!"

Section D

Pay Attention to Key Ideas and Words

An important part of our family vacations was picture taking. It wasn't just fun while we were on the road, it also brought a great deal of enjoyment after we returned home.

As soon as we got our film developed, we would flip through the stack of photographs. Here was a shot of a family member ... or a scenic view ... or an interesting person we met. It is said a picture is worth a thousand words, and we always seemed to require about that many to talk about each picture.

Words are like pictures. Words sum up parts of the world. Think about words such as *lion, ball, running, jealousy, smile*. Words are, in a way, snapshots that put us in mind of still other words. They can be strung together to express thoughts even as thousands of still photos, when put together properly, make a movie.

In reading, we should *pay attention to key ideas and words*. It's like freezing a movie in mid-projection to consider important frames. Through an examination of key words, we can delve more deeply into significant ideas.

The prime tool for biblical word study is a concordance. Concordances list words and the Bible verse references (or short quotations of the verses) in which the words are used. People often reach for concordances when they can remember the gist of a passage but can't recall its location. If you can't remember where to find "for God so loved the world," look up a key word like *loved* or *world* and even a small concordance will tell you that the reference is John 3:16.

But concordances can do more than simply help us locate Bible passages. In fact, the concordance—specifically a complete or unabridged concordance—is probably the most important Bible study tool. Such concordances permit us to scan the Scriptures and find out how and where words are used.

Concordance study enables us to fill in our mental pictures of what various words mean, enriching our Bible reading. In the next two chapters, we will do a bit of this kind of study.

Chapter 9

Christian and Other Interesting Words

Read Acts 11:19–30 as well as the portions of Acts noted throughout this chapter

Which words should we look up in a concordance? Which words should we consider to help us read Acts? These are important questions. Some words have a greater variety of meanings and a richer history of usage than others. A similar thing can happen with pictures. A photo of the White House gets more attention after a vacation than a snapshot of a gas station down the street from the White House.

Choosing Words to Study

Which words should we choose to study? As we noted in the last section, we should *pay attention to what is repeated.* This suggestion can be helpful, to a point, when selecting key words for study. The most frequently used words in the Bible (such as *God* or *Jesus*) are certainly worthy of study. But if you are just starting to work with a concordance, don't turn to these words right away. I make this suggestion because of the sheer volume of references. Can you imagine how much information would confront you if you studied every verse in the Bible that contains the word *Lord?* It would be overwhelming even if you confined your study to the references in Acts. It would be a great topic but probably not one suited to the beginner.

Fortunately, there are other criteria that can help us select words for concordance study. Sometimes we can identify a key word because it is used at important points in the text. For instance, Acts includes a number of internal summaries, passages in which the progress of the Gospel is summed up. We have encountered two such verses in our reading so far. Acts 6:7 says, "And the Word of God grew and the number of the disciples in Jerusalem multiplied greatly, and a great crowd of the priests became obedient to the faith." And Acts 9:31 says, "So the church through all Judea and Galilee and Samaria experienced peace. As it was edified and walked in the fear of the Lord and in the comfort of the Holy Spirit, it was multiplied." Two words that leap out from these summaries are *word* and *church.* And if we checked the remaining summary statements in Acts, we'd find the same emphasis on the *Word* of God (12:24; 19:20) and the *church* (16:5).

The strategic placement of *word* and *church* in these summary statements makes them prime candidates for concordance study. But *word* is used 47 times in Acts! I think we should look for something more manageable. Even *church,* which occurs 21 times in Acts, might not provide the best place to start.

A Study of *Name*

Instead, let's briefly examine the word *name.* We

already have encountered most of its appearances in Acts. It is used 38 times, but in some cases it indicates a human being's name. More often, and more interesting, *name* in Acts is a reference to God's name or, specifically, to Jesus' name. Used in this way, it is an important word that can take us further in our journey through Acts.

As we consider the word *name*, we might use as our starting point the passage Peter quoted from Joel in his Pentecost sermon: All those who call on the *name* of the Lord, the name above every name (Philippians 2:9), are saved (2:21), be they Gentiles or persecutors like Saul (22:16). Then we can look at other passages that link salvation to the Lord's name.

- His *name* was called over them in baptism (2:38; see 15:17 and James 2:7).

- Through Jesus' *name* everyone who believes in Him receives forgiveness of sins (10:43; see Psalm 79:9; 1 John 2:12).

- There is "no other *name* under heaven, given among men, by which we must be saved" (4:12; see Psalm 54:1).

Jesus' *name* is God's power unto salvation. The whole Gospel is wrapped up in it.

The word *name* can refer to the Lord revealing Himself to people, graciously helping and saving them (Exodus 33:19).

- The Good News is about both the kingdom of God and the *name* of Jesus Christ (8:12).

- The *name* of Jesus healed the sick (3:6, 16; see 16:18).

- By this *name,* God did signs and wonders (4:30).

Interestingly, in some passages, God's *name* is none other than God Himself. For example, He took from among the Gentiles a people for His *name* (15:14), a name for which Christians live (15:26) and die (21:13). The Lord said that Saul of Tarsus was "My chosen vessel to bear My *name* before Gentiles and kings and the sons of Israel. For I will show him what it is necessary for him to suffer for the sake of My *name*" (9:15–16). Jesus' name was far more than just a "handle," and it certainly was not a magic formula, as the sons of Sceva learned (19:13–16).

So strong is the association in Acts between the Lord and His name that in some places the text does not specify precisely whose name is being discussed. But the reference is clear anyway.

- Christians at Damascus were amazed at the conversion of Saul, the persecutor of the people in Jerusalem who had called upon "this *name*" (9:21).

- The apostles rejoiced that they were counted worthy to suffer dishonor for the sake of "the *name*" (5:41).

Passages of this sort might seem strange if we did not know, from study elsewhere in Acts, what the word *name* can mean. But when we have done our concordance work, they make sense.

A Study of *Way*

Now, let's turn our attention to another interesting word, *way*. This word comes up in Acts half as often as *name,* but some of its occurrences also might strike us as a bit odd if we have not done some concordance study.

The word *way* often refers to a physical path or road and sometimes to a pattern of conduct. Our eyes pick up nothing surprising about these uses. On the other hand, we also read that Saul of Tarsus set out for Damascus to arrest "those who were of the *Way*" (9:2). Later, he admitted that he had "persecuted this *Way*" (22:4). In Ephesus the apostle Paul encountered problems with those who "slandered the *Way*" (19:9; see 19:23).

How is the word *way* being used in these references? At Paul's hearing before the Roman governor Felix, it becomes clear that the word *way* in such references is equivalent to saying *Christianity* (24:14, 22), but not in an organizational or institutional sense. As Acts 18:25–26 shows, it is "the *Way* of the Lord." Everything fits into place when we remember that Jesus called Himself the *Way*, the Truth, and the Life. "No one comes to the Father except through Me," He said (John 14:6), because He is the *Way*. Those who are "of the *Way*," then, are those who come to the Father through Jesus Christ, by the power of the Holy Spirit.

A Study of *Christian*

We need to add one final word to the parade we have been studying. It is used only twice in Acts, but it is important because of how it stuck. The word is *Christian.*

Christian was first used at Antioch (11:26)—at that time the third-largest city in the Roman world. Antioch was the first urban center to feel the impact of mission to the Gentiles.

As you can see in a good Bible dictionary or Bible atlas—also excellent study tools—Antioch was located almost at the northeastern corner of the Mediterranean Sea. The city buzzed with communication and commerce. It was a cosmopolitan place.

At Antioch it was not Jewish followers of the Way from Jerusalem who started speaking the Good News to the Greek population, but those from Cyprus and Cyrene (11:20). It has been pointed out that the names of these believers have been lost to the historical record. But with the Gospel message in mind and Christ's love in their hearts, they did what Peter had been so slow to do in Acts 10. They reached out to the Gentiles with the Good News.

This was a key moment. Once the Gospel was proclaimed among the Gentiles at an international crossroads like Antioch, there simply would have been no way to keep it bottled up among the Jews, even if the church had wanted to. But thank God the church had heard the Lord's directive. It did not want to contain the Gospel. Barnabas was sent to Antioch from Jerusalem not to scold the brethren, but to encourage them. After he sized up the immensity of the task of nurturing these converts, he brought Saul (about whom Acts had said nothing since his conversion) to Antioch. They labored together for a year in this important location (11:22–26). Antioch was well situated to become the point of departure for Christian outreach to the Gentile world, including the missionary journeys of Paul (13:2–4).

No doubt the Greek converts from many different backgrounds and religions stuck out like the proverbial sore thumb when they became followers of the Way in Antioch and "called on the name of the Lord." Their neighbors, perhaps partly out of confusion or maybe as an insult, gave them the nickname *Christians.*

We bear the name to this day. It may have been coined as an insult, but it does describe us. Truly, we are people who bear our Lord's name. *Christ*ians follow Jesus, the Christ, the Messiah promised long ago. We are "little christs," as Martin Luther liked to point out.

I have ministered to hundreds of people who, like myself, have come to call on the name that is above every name. Completely by the grace of God, we have become followers of the Way who happily bear the name *Christian.* Many of these people already stand in the presence of the Lamb. The victory is fully theirs. For others of us, living and sharing the faith remains a daily challenge and privilege.

Speaking to Paul, King Herod Agrippa II said, "Do you think you can persuade me to be a *Christian* so quickly?" (26:28). This quote includes the second and last place where *Christian* appears in Acts. Of course, we don't persuade, and neither did Paul. The Holy Spirit does that. But we do invite people into our family. And we prominently display our name, even to the ends of the earth. As we do, may God continue to bless us.

Chapter 10

The Holy Spirit

Read the portions of Acts noted throughout this chapter

In the last chapter, we worked on the suggestion to *pay attention to key ideas and words.* We even managed to get our feet wet with a few forays into simple concordance study. Among its other advantages, such word study can bring a refreshing change of pace as we contemplate Scripture. In your ongoing Bible reading, you may cover a certain amount of the biblical text, then linger over some of the words you encountered along the way. This is one technique that will help open up the riches that our Lord gave us when He moved the apostles and prophets to write His Word.

In the previous chapter, we tried not to investigate words that occur with great frequency in Acts. Now we'll try something more challenging. Let's turn to an oft-repeated term (actually, a two-word name). It will challenge us more than the words we discussed because it occurs often in Acts. Its frequent use shows its importance, especially in Acts. We cannot close our concordances without looking at it. On this journey through Acts, we have reached a mandatory side trip.

But it doesn't lie too far to the side. The term we need to look at is *Holy Spirit.*

A Study of *Holy Spirit*

Holy Spirit is used in Acts more than 50 times—more than any word we studied in the last chapter. Most of these occurrences are in Acts 1–12. Of course, the term is a proper name, not a generic word. Therefore, this chapter's examination of *Holy Spirit* will not be a simple word study. Instead, we find ourselves considering a Person, the third person of the Holy Trinity (5:3–4).

The Spirit and Christ

First, it is good to notice the close relationship between the Holy Spirit and our Lord Jesus Christ. Acts tells us that Jesus was anointed with the Holy Spirit (10:38). While He was visibly present with the disciples during the 40 days after Easter, He taught them through the Holy Spirit (1:2). And it was the ascended Christ who poured out the Holy Spirit on Pentecost (2:33). The Spirit spoke to the apostles just as Jesus did (10:13–20). "He will glorify Me," Jesus had predicted concerning the Spirit (John 16:14). In Acts, the Holy Spirit certainly showed Himself to be the "Spirit of Jesus" (16:7; see 5:9).

Not only is the Holy Spirit the promise of the Father (1:4), He is also Jesus' gift to the church (Luke 24:49). As we have noted, Peter said on Pentecost, "Repent and be baptized, each of you, in the name of Jesus Christ for the forgiveness of your sins, and you will receive *the gift of the Holy Spirit*" (2:38, emphasis added). The phrase "the gift of the Holy Spirit" probably means the gift is none other than the Holy Spirit. In a similar way, when we speak of the "city of St. Louis," we mean the city that *is* St. Louis. So the Spirit comes as a gift. He is not to be bought and sold (8:19–20). He can be resisted or refused (7:51), but He cannot be earned by our works.

The Spirit's Work

It also is interesting to note that in the Pentecost prophecy from Joel, the pouring out of the Holy Spirit would lead to the speaking of God's Word (2:17, quoting Joel 2:28). Acts reinforces this point (2:18) and tells us that Christians who were filled with the Holy Spirit spoke the Word with boldness (2:4; 4:31; see 4:8; 6:3, 10; 9:17, 20), both in judgment on sin (13:9–11) and with encouragement for the church (11:22–24).

During Old Testament times, people such as David (1:16; 4:25) and Isaiah (28:25) had been spokesmen for the Spirit as He inspired them to write the Scriptures, the Word of God. By the Spirit, Agabus—a New Testament prophet—predicted a coming famine (11:28). Later he announced Paul's forthcoming arrest in Jerusalem, saying, "Thus says the Holy Spirit ..." (21:11). This prediction further specified what the Holy Spirit already had told Paul—that chains and troubles would await him wherever he went (20:23). In short, the Holy Spirit communicates.

I have always enjoyed the fact that the Spirit told Philip to join the Ethiopian (8:29). Then He whisked

Philip to another place after the Ethiopian was baptized (8:39–40). The Spirit told Peter that the messengers sent by Cornelius were looking for him (10:19–20; see 11:12). He also told the church at Antioch to set apart Barnabas and Saul for missionary travel (13:2). It also was the Holy Spirit who kept Paul and his companions from going to Asia and Bithynia because He had another destination in mind (16:6ff). Paul decided "in the Spirit" (19:21) to go to Jerusalem. Later, he said that he was "bound in the Spirit" to do this despite troubles and even chains (20:22–23). Acts clearly states that the Spirit guided the mission efforts of the church. And He continues to guide them today.

But it doesn't stop there. As Jesus promised (John 14:16–17), the Spirit comforted the church (9:31), helping it bear up under persecution (4:29–31), even in the face of death (7:55–56). The letter sent by the Jerusalem Council to the largely Gentile church of Antioch contained the remarkable words, "It seemed good to the Holy Spirit and us" (15:28), which shows how the Lord guides His church. The Holy Spirit worked through His church to send missionaries (13:2–4) and call pastors (20:28). It doesn't take much study of Acts to see that the Holy Spirit constantly works in the church.

The Importance of the Holy Spirit

Perhaps the most mysterious passage in Acts on the Holy Spirit is the story of Paul's meeting with some "disciples" in Ephesus. Paul asked whether they had received the Holy Spirit when they were converted. They replied that they had never heard of the Holy Spirit. Paul asked, "Into what then were you baptized?" They answered, "Into the baptism of John" (19:1–3).

If their response seems strange, it's probably because John the Baptizer had spoken about the Holy Spirit during his ministry (Luke 3:16). The answers given by these disciples struck Paul as strange too. Had these people been baptized by John the Baptizer? While it was possible that Paul could meet people in Ephesus who had been baptized by John more than 20 years earlier in Palestine, it was highly unlikely. And if these disciples had indeed been baptized by John, would all 12 have so completely forgotten his preaching?

Or had they been baptized by the disciples of John, as apparently was the case for Apollos (18:25)? Or had they been baptized by Apollos? These prospects are more fathomable, but we must not forget that Acts presents Apollos in contrast to these disciples. In other words, they were different. They had *never heard* of the Holy Spirit, but Apollos was "bubbling over with the Spirit" (a possible translation of 18:25). Apollos accurately taught about Jesus (as St. Paul did; see 28:31), but Paul felt it necessary to inform the disciples about Jesus, the one who came after John (19:4). Finally, there is no account of Apollos being rebaptized, whether by Priscilla and Aquila or by anyone else. Paul baptized these disciples (19:5). All in all, we might say the disciples at Ephesus did not have what Apollos had.

The best explanation is that the Ephesian disciples probably had been baptized by people who claimed to be John's followers but who did not know about the Holy Spirit. Accordingly, they had been baptized with a false baptism, despite what they had been told.

So who exactly had been the teacher of these disciples? Who had baptized them and what misinformation had they been given about the Lord? There are no answers to these questions on this side of heaven, nor do we need these answers. Acts does not say that Paul sought answers to these questions (19:4–5). From a pastoral point of view, Paul followed good, loving wisdom as he related to these disciples. Today, prudence indicates that if doubt arises about whether someone has been baptized with a true Christian baptism, the person should be baptized.

The result of this discussion in Acts 19 is striking. Once again, as if to show Paul and the rest of the church that the preaching of the Gospel to the Gentiles was a move in the right direction, the Holy Spirit came on them in a marvelous way. In this case, we also might say the church learned that it was okay to reach out to people with theologically questionable backgrounds.

Acts says that Paul's new friends spoke in tongues (19:6) just as Christians in Jerusalem did on Pentecost (Acts 2) and just as the newly converted Gentiles did at Caesarea (Acts 10). But we note in Acts 19, once again, that there is no promise or prediction that others could expect to experience the same thing.

The Holy Spirit and the Believer

As we wrap up this chapter in our journey together, we can safely conclude that the Holy Spirit is far from unknown in Acts. He is mentioned again and again. He comes as a gift given by the ascended Lord to His church, glorifying Christ as He guides and prompts the church in its efforts to proclaim the saving Gospel.

As Martin Luther says in the *Large Catechism:*

> The Holy Spirit reveals and proclaims that Word; He uses it to shed His light into human hearts and set them aglow; He empowers them to grasp the Word, accept it, cling to it, and faithfully stay with it. For where He does not cause the Word to be proclaimed and to be grasped as the living truth within the heart, all is lost. *(Janzow, p. 73; LC II 42–43)*

This is why I appreciate the memorable explanation of the Third Article in Luther's *Small Catechism:*

> I believe that I cannot by my own reason or strength believe in Jesus Christ, my Lord, or come to Him; but the Holy Spirit has called me by the Gospel, enlightened me with His gifts, sanctified and kept me in the true faith. In the same way He calls, gathers, enlightens, and sanctifies the whole Christian church on earth, and keeps it with Jesus Christ in the one true faith. In this Christian church He daily and richly forgives all my sins and the sins of all believers. On the Last

Day He will raise me and all the dead, and give eternal life to me and all believers in Christ. This is most certainly true.

It *is* most certainly true for us. It is why we say daily, "Thanks, God, for the work of Your Holy Spirit among us. And thanks, God, that this same Spirit gives us the high honor of confessing, praying, singing, and speaking the Master's Word in the Master's name!" Yes, for this great gift, thanks be to God to the ends of the earth.

PART II: SUGGESTIONS FOR READING NARRATIVE

Section E

Pay Attention to Important Characters and Their Actions

As we took family vacations, we liked to observe people. We met an old banjo player who really knew how to make his banjo sing. We had a tour guide at a national park who had more stories to tell than we could ever listen to on one trip. Yes, our vacations were marked by the impact of individuals. People are important.

Thus far in our journey through Acts, we have mentioned people—Peter, Paul, Stephen, Philip. We've looked at the organization of Acts and how these people are included. Now we will focus more closely on the actions of a couple of key people.

It's fitting that this change in focus comes as we are almost halfway through Acts. Now in the second half of our journey, I'd like to draw your attention to several guiding principles for reading narrative accounts such as Acts. Because historical narratives like Acts are concerned with people, the first principle we will consider is *pay attention to important characters and their actions.*

When we speak of "characters," you may wonder whether we are treating Acts as a work of fiction, like a Sherlock Holmes mystery in which the reader encounters the characters of Holmes and Watson, to name just two. Unfortunately, much contemporary biblical scholarship deals with the Bible as nothing more than a story. Sadly, much of this thinking would consider it beside the point, or even absurd, to regard scriptural stories as true, so long as they can be appreciated as carefully crafted and religiously significant.

But this is absolutely *not* the perspective from which we approach Acts. The story is true. It is what it purports to be: history, not fiction, recorded for us by Luke, who not only witnessed many of these events (see the "we" sections, 16:10–17; 20:5–16; 21:1–18; 27 and 28) but was guided by the Holy Spirit to write these words (2 Timothy 3:16; 2 Peter 1:20–21). And these words serve both as a historical record and for our personal edification in the Lord.

When I refer to characters, I do not mean imaginary persons made up by a writer. I am talking about real people through whom the Lord worked. Similarly, one could speak of the characters in the American Revolution—real persons, such as George Washington or Paul Revere, around whom momentous actions and events revolved.

Two people emerge as pivotal historical characters in Acts: Peter and Paul. The next two chapters will explore the lives of those men.

Chapter 11

Peter

Read Acts 9:32–43; 12:1–25; and the portions
of Acts noted throughout the chapter

As you have no doubt noticed, we are not studying the acts of *all* the apostles. Roughly half of Acts (1–12) highlights words and actions of Peter and his associates while the remaining half (13–28) centers on Paul and his associates. In this chapter we will focus on Peter.

Before we get started, consider this: Acts was written selectively. As in the case of the gospel according to St. John, there was undoubtedly much more material available for Acts than what was recorded through divine inspiration (John 20:30). The events recorded in Acts, like those in John, are there to make a point (John 20:31). If we wonder why Acts devotes so much attention to Peter or to Paul, we may not find as clear-cut a statement as the reader of John has in John 20:30–31. But whatever hints we do find in the text will help us understand Acts better.

The Many Sides of Peter

Peter stood out as a leader among the apostles and of the early church (see 1:15–22; 5:1–11). He was a man of compassion (3:6) used powerfully by the Lord both in word (2:36–40; 4:8–13, 18–20; 5:29–32) and in deed (5:15). He never forgot where the real power came from, as shown by his words to Aeneas, "Jesus Christ heals you" (9:34). Time and again in Acts we see Peter strengthening his brethren as Jesus had told him to do (Luke 22:31–32). When Tabitha died, the Christians at Joppa immediately sent word to Peter, and through him the Lord brought her back from death (9:36–41).

There was no question that the work the Lord did through Peter held great importance, even for the enemies of the Way. Once, King Herod Agrippa I had Peter arrested around Passover and handed him over to the soldiers. The circumstances were beginning to look like those surrounding Jesus' death, if not the death of John's brother James (the first of the original 12 to meet with martyrdom). Agrippa detailed an extraordinarily heavy force to guard Peter (12:1–5). But the Lord miraculously released him from prison. Even Peter was surprised by this turn of events (12:6–11).

Peter was beloved by the early Christians. After his release from Agrippa's jail, he went to the home of John Mark's mother and knocked at the door. Rhoda, the maid, was so glad to hear his voice that she ran to tell everyone that Peter was all right, but she forgot to let him in (12:12–18)!

The main picture of Peter painted in Acts, however, is not that of Peter the leader, the friend, or the person in the spotlight. Like the other apostles, Peter was a witness to the risen Christ. Understandably, then, in Acts he appears above all as a man through whom the Master proclaimed His Gospel. Peter does not get the spotlight. Jesus does. In this capacity, Peter forms a good model for us.

Peter Proclaims Prophecy Fulfilled

Already in his Pentecost sermon, Peter spoke of prophecy and fulfillment, which became a well-used method as he and others proclaimed Christ. Peter quoted at length from Psalm 16, which says that God would not let His Holy One suffer decay or leave Him in the grave (Psalm 16:10, quoted in Acts 2:27). Peter added that David did not speak these words about himself because "his grave is with us to this day" (2:29). Instead, Peter said that David knew about, and was speaking specifically concerning, the resurrection of Christ (2:30–31).

In other places Peter called attention to Christ's fulfillment of prophecy (3:18, 21; 10:42–43), proving that God keeps His Word. Peter told the crowds that God promised to send a prophet like Moses "from among your brethren," and He made good on that promise when He sent Jesus (Deuteronomy 18:15ff, quoted in Acts 3:22–23). Peter reminded his listeners that God promised that in Abraham's "Seed" all the families of the earth would be blessed (Genesis 12:3, quoted in Acts 3:25). Peter declared that this Seed was none other than Jesus (Galatians 3:16).

Another important Messianic prophecy that Peter reflected upon is Isaiah 52:13–53:12, although he did not quote it as extensively as we find, for example, in Acts 8:32–33. This "Servant song" described the Messiah as the Servant who, because of

God's will (Isaiah 53:10), suffers and dies in place of His people (see Isaiah 53:4–8) only to be vindicated in the end (see Isaiah 53:11–12; 52:13, 15). Peter brought this prophecy to mind for his hearers by calling Jesus God's "Servant" in Acts 3:13, 26.

If we think of Peter's past, we may remember how Peter recoiled at the thought of Jesus' suffering (Matthew 16:21–23). Now, in light of the resurrection victory, could it be that the Lord was using Peter's memory of his objection and Jesus' answer to help him cherish and proclaim an Old Testament prophecy that emphasized the Messiah's suffering? God used the personalities and experiences of His inspired writers as He committed His Word to writing.

Peter Proclaims the Resurrection

The resurrection of Christ became a major emphasis in Peter's preaching. As in Psalm 16, the resurrection shows that the Lord had been in charge all along and that Jesus' enemies had not won. Jesus had. The Isaiah 53 prophecy already indicated that the Suffering Servant would at length be given life again and exalted (Isaiah 53:11–12). Jesus, God's holy and righteous servant, was vindicated after all.

Recently, a friend went through a rough time. He and his wife had to put their dog to sleep. Two weeks later, my friend had a dream in which he came home from work to find his wife with their beloved dog, healthy and happy. In the dream, his wife was trying to explain this surprise, but the main thing on his mind was the return of his dog. Tears of joy filled his eyes. He told his wife, "I have to tell everyone at work about this. I may even bring our dog to work with me!" Then he woke up from the dream.

Consider the loss the disciples experienced when Jesus died. Peter, in particular, must have been distraught. Not only had he denied Jesus (Luke 22:54–62) after proudly boasting that he wouldn't (Matthew 26:33, 35), but now he would have to go on without Jesus to guide him in the way of life (John 6:68) and save him from his sin (Luke 5:8–10) and unbelief (Matthew 14:28–31). What joy Peter must have felt when Jesus came back, not to accuse and condemn him for his failures and sins, but to forgive him and to be his Rock and his Lord again. With Jesus back, Peter went from the dumps to the heights. Now he had everything!

Peter Proclaims Forgiveness

Peter carried this same message of forgiveness in his sermons recorded in Acts. Peter aimed not only to show people their sin, but more important, to show them their risen and victorious Savior. The Lord Jesus who forgave Peter the denier could forgive anyone— including those who had denied Christ when Pilate wanted to release Him (3:13–14).

From the cross Christ had spoken words of forgiveness: "Father, forgive them for they do not know what they are doing" (Luke 23:34). Peter began turning this forgiveness of Christ toward the temple crowd when he said, "And now, brothers, I know that you acted in ignorance" (3:17).

Jesus' resurrection was God's declaration that the sins of the world had been paid for, that in Christ there is forgiveness for everyone. Because of Jesus our sins are, literally, wiped out (3:19) by God. In Christ there is forgiveness and salvation for us too (see 2:38; 4:12; 5:31; 10:43).

This may seem too good to be true, especially when we think of all the ways we have failed our God and sinned against Him. But it *is* true. As we have noted, Acts does not simply tell us a nice story with a happy ending. It holds before our eyes the great historical truth of a Savior, our Savior, who came, lived, died, and rose again that we might forever be forgiven before our Triune God!

Here lies the big difference between my friend's dream about his dog and Jesus' appearances to Peter. In Peter's case it was no dream. Besides Peter, many others saw Jesus alive after He had died. Christ ate with them and taught them, not once but several times. They saw Him, off and on, throughout the 40 days before He ascended. As Peter later wrote, "We did not follow cleverly devised myths when we made known to you the power and coming of our Lord Jesus Christ, but we were eyewitnesses of His majesty" (2 Peter 1:16).

Why Speak Out?

It was the most natural thing in the world for Peter and the others to speak about what had happened. Jesus had instructed them to do so, of course, but even if He had never mentioned it, they hardly could have contained themselves. Like my friend, they would have been moved by a joyful impulse to share their good news, even without a divine mandate to do so.

Thank God that by His grace this is the same Gospel and the same impulse that we have. Even if Jesus never had said that we should tell others what He has done, I would want to do it. I suspect you would too. But the Lord has told us to share the Good News. Through Peter, He instructs Christians to be ready at all times to speak of our hope (1 Peter 3:15).

In his dream, my friend said, "I have to tell everyone about this. I may even bring our dog to work." Our Lord Jesus is risen from the dead, and He goes with us wherever we go. At work, at play, at home, you name it—we daily have the fantastic joy and privilege of bringing Jesus to people when we tell them about Him. This was Peter's life-changing joy, and we share in it too.

Chapter 12

Paul

Read Acts 13–14

From its beginning, Acts 13 puts us in mind of how our good and gracious God works through people. It names several prophets and teachers at Antioch. This is the first list of Christians since the early days of the church in Jerusalem (1:13; 6:5). Now the church has expanded to Gentile territory, and it will soon move into another area of mission endeavor as Barnabas and Saul are set apart for mission work by the church of Antioch (13:2) and sent by the Holy Spirit (13:4).

Paul Steps to the Forefront

In Acts 13 and 14 we find the story of Paul's first missionary journey. At this time, Paul emerges as a pivotal figure in the first-century church. Not long after the trip started, Paul stepped to the forefront. In Acts 13:9, he is identified by his Roman name, Paul, in addition to his Jewish name, Saul. By Acts 13:13 we read not of Barnabas and Saul, but of "Paul and those with him." Some believe John Mark left the missionaries as soon as they arrived on the mainland from Cyprus (13:13) because he had become upset with how Paul was overshadowing his relative Barnabas.

Even on this first trip, we begin to see hints of how Paul's missionary career would progress. Roman items and references are prominent in Acts 13. The apostle became better known by his Roman name than his Jewish name. A prominent convert on Cyprus was the Roman proconsul, Sergius Paulus. The first city in which we have a record of Paul's preaching, another Antioch, was a Roman colony where imperial army veterans had settled. As the Lord arranged these events and inspired Luke to record them, Paul was bringing the Gospel not just to Gentiles in general, but to Romans in particular.

Paul's Similarities to Peter

Although Paul was coming into his own, he was very much like Peter, even in the things he did. For example, in Acts 14:8–10 there is an account of Paul healing a crippled man, which could be compared to a similar story involving Peter in Acts 3:1–10. In both cases, the man had been crippled from birth; the apostle looked at him and spoke; the man got up and walked immediately without needing to learn how to use the new strength in his legs. Again, as the Lord arranged events and inspired Luke to record them, the implication is that Paul's apostolic call was no less legitimate than Peter's. Thus, the church's mission continued to progress as the Lord wanted it to progress. Jesus was still carrying out His work through this "new" apostle, Paul, in all the places where the first missionary journey took him.

Paul Proclaims Like Peter

The main subject of Acts 13 is Paul's first recorded sermon. In some ways this address is more remarkable for what it did not say than for what it did say. Addressing a Jewish synagogue audience, Paul might have focused on his personal history as a devotee of the law and his dramatic encounter with the risen Christ on the road to Damascus. We already have seen that Paul was quite capable of talking about such matters at an appropriate time and place. But in approaching the Jews as a missionary, Paul thought it more vital to preach Christ than to recount the details of his conversion.

As one who has preached many sermons, I have come to understand the importance of Paul's decision. While I have never eliminated all personal references from my preaching, I always enter a pulpit with this thought from John the Baptizer in mind: I desire that, as a result of this sermon, Christ may increase and I decrease (John 3:30).

Paul's preaching bore a striking resemblance to Peter's. His remarks were steeped in Old Testament history (13:16b–25) and prophecy (13:26–41). Like Peter, Paul proclaimed the Gospel in terms of promise and fulfillment. Also like Peter, Paul spoke of how Jesus had been hanged on a tree (13:29; compare 5:30; 10:39). Behind this choice of words lies the statement in Deuteronomy 21:23 that everyone who hangs on a tree is cursed before God.

I wonder whether those who heard this sermon later recalled this choice of words when they read Paul's letter to the Galatians. This epistle was quite likely addressed to this audience and to Christians elsewhere in the region. In it, Paul quoted Deuteronomy and said that Christ became a curse for us in our place (Galatians 3:13). Notice how strong this language is. It does not say that Christ became *like* a curse or even that He *bore* a curse. Christ *became* a curse, it says, as God held Him guilty of all the sin of all people of all time. Jesus did this for us too. He died our accursed death under the wrath of God.

Finally, and again like Peter, Paul stressed the resurrection of Christ. Since He was the man who is also God (13:33, which quotes Psalm 2:7), Jesus could not remain dead after He paid for the sins of the world. He had to live. He was the very "Author of life" as Peter had put it (3:15). In a point similar to the one made by Peter on Pentecost, Paul noted that Christ as the true Holy One did not experience corruption in the grave (13:35–37; see 2:25–31).

"Through this one, forgiveness of sins is proclaimed to you," Paul concluded, "and in Him every one who believes is freed [literally, *justified*] from all the things from which you could not be freed by the law of Moses" (13:38–39). Here we find another preview of things to come as Paul employed the language of justification by grace apart from works of the law at the very climax of his sermon.

Reaction to Paul

Paul's note of grace resonated among the people. A week later, Luke tells us, almost the whole city wanted to hear more of this message (13:44). Then opposition arose from staunch Jews. This would not be the last time Paul would encounter such resistance.

With Barnabas, Paul responded. They said, "It was necessary that the Word of God be spoken to you first. Since you throw it aside and judge yourselves unworthy of eternal life, behold, we are turning to the Gentiles" (13:46). This became a pattern for Paul: First, he went to the synagogue, then wherever else he could be heard. When the Gentiles heard the Gospel, Acts says that "as many as were appointed for eternal life believed" (13:48).

We should linger for a moment over the truth set forth in these two short verses from Acts 13. On one hand, God receives all the glory for the conversion of the Gentiles. The fact that they believed is not credited to their superior intelligence, fervor, or some greater receptivity to the message. Their faith was solely because of God and His work. On the other hand, Paul and Barnabas told the unbelieving Jews in no uncertain terms that their unbelief was their fault, not God's. Throughout Paul's career, we repeatedly see this emphasis on God's free grace for all people. As Paul wrote to the Romans, "I am not ashamed of the Gospel, for it is the power of God for salvation to everyone who believes, first the Jew and also the Greek" (Romans 1:16).

No Pedestals for Paul

After some time at Iconium, the missionaries arrived at Lystra, where Paul healed the crippled man (14:8–10). This event caused quite a sensation, owing in part to a bit of local mythology. For years the story had been told in Lystra that two Greek gods, Zeus and Hermes, once visited that area in human form. When Paul healed the crippled man, the people concluded the gods were back. They did not want to miss welcoming Zeus and Hermes (14:11–14). In fact, the priest of Zeus was ready to offer a sacrifice to Paul and Barnabas! "Why are you doing these things?" Paul asked the crowd. "We are men, like you in every way" (14:15). Paul and Barnabas were bringing the people the Good News of Christ. But most of Paul's speech at Lystra, as it is recorded in Acts, was devoted to preventing the people from treating him and Barnabas as gods.

I don't know how much danger exists that modern congregations will treat their pastors as gods. But there's an important lesson for the church in the events at Lystra. Pastors are ambassadors of Jesus Christ. They hold an office instituted by the Lord Himself. As they carry out the duties of this office, they bring the Good News to their congregations and to many others. But as Paul pointed out, they are not the personal presence of the divine in the world, not even of the true God.

As Paul said, they are men, like everyone else in every way. They have strengths and weaknesses. They can be tempted. They sin. They, too, need the forgiving grace of God in Jesus Christ on a daily basis. And as Paul learned only too well, they also can be mistreated. Before he left Lystra—a city whose inhabitants wanted to worship him at first—Paul was stoned and left for dead (14:19–20; see 2 Corinthians 11:25).

Jesus Continues to Work through People

I often marvel that the Lord of the church does His work through people because people are fallible. They can and do make mistakes. And sometimes when a person does the right thing, he or she is mistreated to the point of giving up. I have seen this among pastors, teachers, missionaries, and among dedicated laypeople.

There are so many ways the progress of the Gospel could have ground to a halt long ago, all because of the weakness and sinfulness of human beings. But this has not happened. The Gospel still goes out through the church and its pastors because every day the ascended Lord Jesus and His Holy Spirit perform the miracles of conversion and preservation in the faith. If God could give Paul and Barnabas the courage to return and strengthen their brethren in cities where they had suffered persecution (14:21–22), think of what He can do and still is doing in us today.

What a privilege God has given us. Peter and Paul were entrusted with a special responsibility to spread the Word. But it is also true that every Christian, in his or her calling, has been given the Gospel, not only to believe but to share. And in such sharing, we are blessed to be part of the work of salvation that the Lord accomplishes through people. He opens doors (Acts 14:27) as His powerful Word is spoken by us. What an ongoing blessing this is.

Section F

Pay Attention to Conflicts

How nice it would be to say there were never any conflicts in our family travel trailer adventures. But as you might expect, to say so would not really be truthful. Nor would it be realistic. You simply cannot put five people into a 17½' travel trailer for two weeks or longer, add occasional rainy spells, and expect to avoid conflicts or misunderstandings. Not in this sinful world.

On our trips, we heard things like this:

- "He spilled his soda on my bed. Now what am I supposed to do?"

- "Who put my shorts on the floor? Look at how dirty they are."

- "Why don't you kids—and you too, Dad—get out of the trailer so I can fix supper? It is just too crowded in here."

- "Who forgot to put the lid on tight on the pickle jar? It came off and now look at this sticky mess in the refrigerator."

Such conflicts are part of five people living together in a confined space. The challenge was to work through such conflicts when they surfaced, resolve them, and move on to enjoy our vacation.

As we move into the next section, we will practice yet another principle that helps us read narrative: *Pay attention to conflicts.* This suggestion complements the principle to pay attention to important characters and their actions.

Like the modern church, the first-century church certainly did not lack people with strong, forceful personalities. There's nothing wrong with this. God gives personalities to us. In the previous section we observed that the Lord worked through people like Peter and Paul to carry out His mission. And He still works through people.

As we live in this fallen world, people come into conflict with one another—even in the church. Often these conflicts become tests of character or even schools for building character. This was certainly the case with the conflicts described in Acts 15. They were far more serious than not putting the lid on the pickle jar. But in these conflicts, we see the guiding hand of the Lord Jesus Christ at work in His church.

Chapter 13

Conflict in the Church

Read Acts 15:1–35

Acts 15 provides an informative look at a very serious conflict in the early church. It also affords insight into how strife was handled in a God-pleasing way. Acts 15 helpfully describes how the early Christians respected one another and listened to one another (15:12). But they decided the issue at hand on its merits and according to God's Word, not by succumbing to personal power plays.

The Conflict Grows

The issue behind the church conflict described in Acts 15 has emerged several times in our reading. It revolved around the new Gentile converts and their status before God. We have seen how difficult it was for the church to reach out to Gentiles. We saw the Lord nudge His church in the direction of mission to the Gentiles in several ways. The two oft-recounted events—Paul's conversion and Peter's experience with Cornelius' family—provided major impetus for mission to the Gentiles.

By the time of Acts 15, the church found itself well established at an international crossroads, Antioch of Syria. Through journeys like the one Paul and

Barnabas had just completed, the Gospel was reaching countless Gentiles. But the misgivings concerning Gentiles showed themselves to be most deeply rooted among certain Jewish Christians. For them, these misgivings constituted an emotional barrier as well as a theological one.

We get a hint of their attitude when we read about the accusation leveled against Peter after his visit to the family of Cornelius. Some Jewish Christians were concerned that Peter entered the house of uncircumcised people and ate with them (11:1–3). Peter responded by describing what happened, including his dream. Luke recorded his words as the second telling of the story of Cornelius and Peter in Acts. Clearly, it was important not only that Peter had reached out to the Gentiles, but that the Jerusalem church could see that this was the right thing to do. At first the accusations of Peter's hearers were silenced. Then they glorified God (11:18).

Evidently not everyone was satisfied, though. At some point after Paul's first missionary journey, unauthorized people came to Antioch from Judea and said, "Unless you are circumcised according to the custom of Moses, you cannot be saved" (15:1; 15:24 reveals that they were unauthorized). These people, sometimes called Judaizers, were claiming that Gentile Christians would have to obey the law (15:5).

Practically speaking, the Judaizers called into question whether mission outreach to the ends of the earth was really a good use of the church's time and energy. Moreover, their message of obedience to the law conflicted with what we have identified as the other side of the coin of mission to the Gentiles: justification by grace for Christ's sake through faith.

No wonder Paul and Barnabas came into conflict with the Judaizers (15:2). (In an unguarded moment, though, Barnabas and Peter were influenced by them to a degree [Galatians 2:11ff].) Quite likely, Paul was spurred at this point to write a letter in defense of justification by grace to the new Christians in the cities that he and Barnabas had visited on their first missionary journey. This was his epistle to the Galatians, now famous as the "declaration of Christian liberty."

Council at Jerusalem

But the problem had grown to such proportions that a single letter could not solve it. A council convened at Jerusalem to face the issue squarely. It immediately becomes apparent from the warm welcome Paul and Barnabas received (15:4) that the apostles and leaders in Jerusalem—as well as the whole church—had not objected to their mission efforts among the Gentiles nor to the theological implications of those efforts for justification by grace, not by works. Instead, the opposition was led by believers from the party of the Pharisees (15:5).

At the council, much debate ensued (15:7) and for good reason. Consider what was at stake. If matters had turned out differently, Christianity might have remained a relatively small movement, attracting only Jews and those Gentiles who would submit to Old Testament ceremonial law. At the same time, and of still greater importance, the Gospel of God's grace in Christ would have been compromised. But thanks be to God, that did not happen.

Christians today have two ways to evaluate a theological idea or teaching. One way is to ask what the idea or teaching does to the Gospel. The other is to ask how it squares with the Scriptures. The apostolic council of Acts 15 provides a single case study of how the church applied both questions to an important issue.

Evaluation Based on the Gospel

Peter took up the first question. In his speech (15:7–11), he briefly recalled the conversion of Cornelius' family (the third and final mention in Acts of the event). God "cleansed their hearts by faith," Peter said (15:9). Anything else would be a return to the dead-end path of salvation by the law. Thus, Peter pleaded, "Why do you put God to the test, placing a burden on the neck of the [Gentile] disciples which neither our fathers nor we ourselves could bear?" (15:10). He concluded, in words that remind us of Paul's epistles, "We believe that we will be saved through the grace of the Lord Jesus, the same way they will" (15:11).

Again we note the theological unity shared by the apostles Peter and Paul. Both taught that anything that contradicts the truth of justification by grace through faith must have no place in the church because the church belongs to the Christ who shed His blood to give salvation freely.

The reformers used this standard in their theological debates. They rejected Rome's sacrifice of the mass as well as prayers to the saints because both conflicted with the teaching about Christ and justification through faith in Him (Tappert, pp. 293, 297; SA II ii 1, 25). We employ this same standard in our church today and must continue to do so in the future.

Mission Update

Next, Paul and Barnabas reported on their missionary work among the Gentiles and the signs and wonders God had done. Like the extraordinary manifestation of the Holy Spirit among the Samaritans described in Acts 8, or the one that occurred when Peter preached to the family of Cornelius as discussed in Acts 10, these signs encouraged the church that mission to the Gentiles was the right move. Interestingly, though, the report of the missionaries does not receive emphasis in Acts 15. It is mentioned in only one verse (15:12).

Evaluation Based on the Scriptures

The decisive word at the apostolic council came from the mouth of James. He was not the brother of John, one of the original 12 disciples. That James already had been killed by Herod Agrippa I (12:2). The James who spoke in Acts 15 was "the Lord's brother," probably born to Joseph and Mary after the virgin birth of Jesus (Galatians 1:19). It seems James had risen to prominence in the Jerusalem church some time back, at least since Acts 12:17. As Jesus' brother, James would have commanded tremendous respect, but he clinched the discussion at the apostolic council not by the force of his personality, but by citing the Scriptures. This is the second way we can evaluate a theological idea or teaching.

James quoted from the end of Amos (Amos 9:11–12), but the entire Old Testament resounds with the thought expressed in those words. Thus, it plays a symphony of support for mission to the Gentiles. Amos predicted a time when Gentiles would be included among God's people, and this time was at hand now that Christ had come. Scripture had the last word. So the issue was settled. Mission to the Gentiles proved to be in accord with God's Word. Any objections to it were waved aside by the apostolic council.

This same method for evaluating theological ideas or teachings—asking how they square with Scripture—holds true for us today. It's possible for any group to convince themselves that all manner of things are compatible with the Gospel, if they lose sight of the Gospel as taught in Scripture.

Putting Mission to the Gentiles into Practice

After finding scriptural support for outreach, James suggested that Gentile Christians be counseled to avoid certain things that had the potential to cause division between them and Jewish Christians (15:20). His suggestions, including abstinence from meat of strangled animals and from blood, were not intended to impose some small measure of ceremonial law on the Gentile Christians anymore than his specifying that the Gentiles avoid unchastity somehow indicates that the church ordinarily would not have considered such a thing sinful. James' suggestions simply were aimed at reducing the most likely tensions between Jewish and Gentile Christians because they were now one people of God in Christ Jesus. The idea was to "avoid offense" (Tappert, p. 92; AC XXVIII 65). The church adopted these sensible suggestions and sent them in a letter to the Christians at Antioch of Syria (15:22–35).

Conflict in the Modern Church

We can learn much from this account in Acts. It is sobering to realize that the early Christian church had problems—especially problems with false doctrine—that needed to be addressed. Strong personalities were involved, then as now, and they no doubt complicated matters. But the personalities were not the deciding factor at the apostolic council.

In the church, we sometimes appear more impressed by *who* said something than by *what* was actually said. Perhaps you have noticed this tendency when certain leaders, experts, or groups speak. I suppose it is an understandable temptation, but we should recognize it for what it is—a temptation. When we give in to it, we ignore how the church functions best, at any level. We forget that we have one Teacher, and we are all members of one family (Matthew 23:8). As long as the church is in the world, there will be the temptation to follow people, not the Lord. Succumbing to this temptation ultimately will cost us the Gospel of Christ. We always need to guard against this.

In Acts 15 we see how the early church dealt with its doctrinal problem. It aired the issues, as Christians listened intently to one another. Then it reached a decision on the controverted teachings in light of the Gospel of justification by grace and of how well the issues squared with the Bible. Finally, it did not hesitate to appeal to Christians to act in certain ways for the sake of love and unity. This presents a good pattern for us to follow, even today.

While Paul was embroiled in the controversy that eventually led to the Jerusalem council described in Acts 15, he wrote about his determination "that the truth of the Gospel be preserved to you" (Galatians 2:5). It is for the sake of the Gospel and for the salvation of people that the church has been called to contend for the faith once delivered to the saints. That is a fact our forefathers recognized and accepted. The same must hold true for us. It is also why we daily ask God to keep us steadfast in the truth of His holy Word.

Chapter 14

Conflict between Christians

Read Acts 15:36–41

On this leg of our journey through Acts, we proceed with clear-eyed realism. As sinners in the midst of a sinful world, we know conflicts inevitably arise. Sometimes they drive us; sometimes they hurt us. As we read about other sinners, including those in the Bible, we notice that it is good to pay attention to conflicts.

The Scriptures are up-front in their discussion of such matters. The Bible is the inspired Word of God, but it harbors no sins among its saints. On its pages we learn much about the various conflicts and troubles that befell Abraham, David, or Peter, often as a result of their personal faults. In the Scriptures, we find that it is true: No one is good but God.

Living the Theology of the Cross

As we have learned, the march of the Gospel into the first-century world forms an extraordinary story filled with faith and marked by the miraculous. But it hardly could be said to have made unimpeded progress. There were many problems and conflicts. The church *proclaimed* the theology of the cross. It also found itself called to *live* the theology of the cross. At times, things must have seemed hopeless. In this fact lies a truly marvelous thing about the church's life, whether then or now. The ascended Lord works to bless us, even despite us.

In the previous chapter, we encountered a conflict ignited by false doctrine. But the early church experienced other conflicts as well, including fightings without and fears within (2 Corinthians 7:5). These had a variety of origins, including the lies of Ananias and Sapphira (5:1–11), the greed of Simon the magician (8:18–24), and the assassination plot that might have ended the apostolic career of Paul just as it was beginning (9:23–25). We could extend the list further, based solely on our reading in Acts to this point. Now we will add another illustration.

Conflict Hurts

In some ways, I find the brief description of a personal conflict at the end of Acts 15 more painful than the longer account of a doctrinal conflict (15:1–35 and elsewhere). This personal conflict split up the missionary team of Paul and Barnabas.

It may at first strike us as a small matter, easily described in a few verses. But think of how large it must have loomed in the mind and heart of Paul, Barnabas, or anyone close to them.

As we have followed their steps thus far in Acts, Paul and Barnabas were brothers, colleagues, and co-workers in Christ. Barnabas had put in a good word for Saul of Tarsus after his conversion when many Christians were understandably fearful of him (9:27). In the account of the first missionary journey (Acts 13–14), the names of these two men were mentioned together routinely—even if as "Barnabas and Saul" at the start and as "Paul and Barnabas" later. Shoulder to shoulder they had labored during the recent doctrinal struggle (15:2, 12), despite a lapse on Barnabas' part on one occasion (Galatians 2:13).

Now, when the time was ripe to celebrate and share the blessing of justification by grace through faith once more by way of another mission thrust into the Gentile world, a disagreement arose between these friends. It turned out to be so pointed that it ended their days of working together (15:39). Conflict between Christians hurts.

Paul vs. Barnabas

The problem arose because Barnabas wanted his kinsman John Mark to accompany them on this second missionary journey, as he had on the first. But Paul did not agree. He remembered that Mark had left them at the earliest opportunity "and did not go along with them to the work" (15:38). Paul probably did not want Mark to start out with them again, only to leave at some later point.

Why did Paul take this position? Several guesses have been ventured. Perhaps Mark had left them because he objected to Paul's stress on reaching out to the Gentiles. Now in the wake of the apostolic council, Paul wanted nothing on the second journey to compromise the mission to the Gentiles. However, this prospect seems unlikely since Mark knew both Paul and Barnabas already had been working among the Gentiles in Antioch.

More plausibly, Mark might have left because he did not like how Paul was beginning to overshadow Barnabas, especially on Barnabas' home turf of Cyprus (4:36). Or maybe Mark simply experienced a failure of nerve, leaving Paul to wonder whether he could be counted on again.

Whatever his reasons, Paul had made up his mind. I wonder whether Mark had any idea, when he left the missionaries in Pamphylia (13:13), the problems his action would cause in the future.

Barnabas was committed to his position too. The apostles called him "Son of Encouragement" (a nickname mentioned in 4:36), and he was surely an active encourager (11:23; see 14:22). Barnabas wanted to encourage Mark, even at the cost of splitting up with Paul. Perhaps Barnabas remembered how he once had encouraged Paul to come and lend a hand in Antioch (11:25), thus positioning Paul for his wide-ranging missionary journeys when God's appropriate time arrived. In any case, Barnabas was no less determined than Paul.

All the ingredients were in place for a tough, heated "church fight." Doctrine seems to have had little or nothing to do with it. The issue was really a question of the wiser way to do the Lord's work: bring Mark along or not? We have many similar conflicts today, and we can learn a few lessons from how Paul and Barnabas handled this one.

Handling Conflict between Christians

First, neither Paul nor Barnabas gave up on Jesus. This is the most important point. They did not allow their "church fight" to sour them on the Lord of the church. Nor did they use this disagreement as an impetus to start looking for doctrinal problems with each other.

Years ago C.F.W. Walther wisely cautioned that personal conflicts in the church can escalate easily into doctrinal controversies. He wrote that once love has been destroyed, it won't be long before one person believes what the other person rejects, and the other teaches what the first considers an error ... . For example, one person takes a stand, and another person takes the opposite stand. Perhaps the one person dislikes the other; he simply can't stand him, and for that reason he inflexibly maintains his position. It is frightening (*schrecklich*) what harm can result when members of a church organization do not vigilantly guard their fraternal love. (*Essays vol. II, p. 56*)

Second, Paul and Barnabas did not allow their disagreement to disrupt the rest of the church. Neither went around pouting about not getting his way. And neither tried to use the occasion to gain power or publicity for himself.

Third, they both kept doing the work to which they had been called. In some respects, things actually turned out better. Now two missionary teams were traveling from Antioch to spread the saving Gospel. Before there had been only one. What might have loomed as a profound embarrassment to the cause of Christ became a definite plus.

When the church loses focus on its mission to proclaim the Gospel to the ends of the earth, the smallest molehills can become towering mountains. Christians can find themselves at one another's throats before they realize what's happening. But when this focus is maintained, as in the case of Paul and Barnabas, remarkable things happen. Satan may have meant the sharp disagreement between Paul and Barnabas for evil, but God meant it for good (Genesis 50:20).

Confidence Through It All

This is the kind of confidence we Christians have in our Lord Jesus Christ, who gave Himself for us so that nothing can separate us from God's love (Romans 8:28–39). Even in the midst of conflict, we can confess our sins to Him and receive His absolution in Word and sacrament. Then we can serve as channels through which His great love flows from us to other people (John 7:38). We can be peacemakers.

Paul emerges as a peacemaker in his "swan song" letter to Timothy. Facing the prospect of execution, he wrote, "Get Mark and bring him with you." Yes, Mark! Paul added that "he is helpful in serving me" (2 Timothy 4:11). Everything that had happened on the first missionary journey and before the second—whatever conflict, problems, and sins there may have been—was forgiven and forgotten in Jesus Christ. What a powerful example!

As a Christian, I pray that I grow in my understanding that, on account of Christ, the sins of my brothers and sisters are no longer theirs to bear. Nor are their sins mine to hang over their heads. Their sins, and mine, were all taken by Jesus to the cross. And He left them there when He rose from the dead.

This is a truth we need to recognize more clearly each day, both in our lives and in the lives of others. It is also a truth we need to live out daily as we find ourselves in conflicts at home or in our congregations. As we live in the reality of overflowing forgiveness, we will model for others the life of Christ. Moreover, we also will direct the attention of others to the saving power of Christ's Gospel in a believer's life. God help us here also.

Section G

Pay Attention to Unexpected Twists

I already have mentioned that careful planning plays an important part in any good vacation. But on our family vacations, we found out that things do not always go as planned.

Once, in the Colorado Rockies, I pulled onto a side road that I thought would lead us to a campground. As the road narrowed, though, it seemed we were not on the right trail. There was no way to back up, especially pulling a trailer, so we kept driving. After several frustrating miles, we came across a wonderful campground next to a stream at the foot of a beautiful mountain range. We fondly remembered that place for many years, partly because we came across it so unexpectedly.

As we continue traveling through Acts, we want to *pay attention to unexpected twists.* Sometimes these twists or surprises take the form of conflict between people, as we have seen. No matter how these twists arise, though, in every case they make their mark on the people in the account. I'm always impressed how our Lord used unexpected and seemingly undesirable events to accomplish His purposes.

When we talk about unexpected twists, it may seem to be a rule for interpreting fiction. After all, the author of a novel has complete control of the yarn being spun. Twists in the plot are carefully contrived to occur precisely at the times when they will exert maximum impact on readers.

As I have pointed out, however, Acts is not a novel. From beginning to end it is *history*. It records events that actually happened. Of course, history writers do not have the freedom fiction writers enjoy. Therefore, some may wonder why I mention the suggestion to pay attention to unexpected twists. They may believe this suggestion will not prove helpful, either for reading Acts or for reading any other account of facts that lie beyond the author's control.

But let us not be so quick to dismiss this suggestion. Even in secular history, unexpected twists arise at critical points. For example, Christopher Columbus set sail in search of a shorter, or at least more direct, route to the East. No one knew when his voyage began that, though never reaching its intended destination, it would put North America on Europe's map of the world. This twist in history, unexpected as it was, was extremely important. A historian writing about it today would likely call attention to it, even though he or she, as the author, did not invent the twist.

Further, in Acts and other biblical histories, the real Author behind the human writer is truly in control, both of the activity described and of the text that describes it. Earlier we remarked on the Lord's arrangement of events and His inspiration of Luke to write about them in Acts. The subject of this section—Paul's second missionary journey—forms another prime example of how God shows Himself to be the author of the church's unfolding mission as well as the historical biblical account of it. His hand is evident here, frequently in the form of unexpected twists.

Almost nothing in the second missionary journey went according to plan—at least not according to the plans and projections of human beings. But through it all, the Lord accomplished exactly what He wanted.

Chapter 15

Not Exactly What Was Expected

Read Acts 16

Acts tells us a great deal about how Paul and others ran into unexpected twists in life and ministry. It also shows how the Holy Spirit turned these occasions into meaningful, blessed opportunities in the Lord.

A New Companion

The unexpected twists of the second missionary journey began as Paul set out to return to cities that he and Barnabas visited on the first missionary journey. Paul probably thought that Barnabas would be traveling at his side when he came back to encourage the Christians in these places. But on this trip, Barnabas was not with him.

Instead, Paul picked up a new companion in the region of Lystra and Derbe—Timothy. Born to a Greek father and a Jewish mother, Timothy had never been circumcised. Paul, the man who contended so strongly at the apostolic council for freedom from the Old Testament law and who was now carrying word of that council's decision (16:4), took the unexpected step of circumcising Timothy (16:3). This was not a matter of necessity but a tactical move that would get

Timothy into the synagogues Paul intended to visit in the days and weeks ahead. Even at this point, years before writing about being all things to all people (1 Corinthians 9:19–23), Paul was putting this wisdom into practice.

A New Destination

Then an even more unexpected thing happened. The Spirit prevented Paul, Timothy, and their colleagues from speaking the Word in certain places.

First, they tried to go west, to the Aegean coast of Asia Minor and its thriving city of Ephesus. Then they tried to move north to the province of Bithynia on the Black Sea. I always have been intrigued that Acts says the Spirit thwarted both attempts, while not specifying precisely how He did so (16:6–7).

At the time, this must have been a genuine disappointment. Paul probably was most eager to introduce the Gospel into either or both of these territories. The work in Asia Minor was hardly finished. But the Lord had other ideas. When Paul and his party arrived at the coastal city of Troas, hardly able to go any farther to the north or to the west while remaining in Asia Minor, Paul had a vision of a man from Macedonia pleading for help (16:8–9). That would be their next destination.

This was an historic moment. For the first time on record, the Gospel reached European soil. Interestingly, centuries later, Asia Minor (modern-day Turkey) came under Islamic domination. During the Middle Ages, the geographic focus of Christianity was not so much there as in Europe—the very place Paul virtually had to be forced to visit. An unexpected twist indeed.

At times we have our hearts set on one thing, but the Lord has something better in mind, so He tells us no. It is not a no of condemnation because "there is now no condemnation for those who are in Christ Jesus" (Romans 8:1). When we experience this fatherly no, we can recall, as Paul said, that "all things work together for good to those who love God, who are called according to His purpose" (Romans 8:28). *All* things. Let me repeat these words because this is something we need to hear very clearly in our lives—*all things!*

Ministry in Philippi

The first Macedonian city of any size Paul and his party went to was Philippi, a Roman colony settled by Roman soldiers. This setting for evangelism was different from anything they had known previously. Paul could not go to the synagogue first—there was no synagogue. The few Jews and God-fearers had only a place of prayer near the river. There the mission work started.

The Lord "opened the heart" of a business-woman named Lydia (16:14). She and her family were baptized, and she opened her home as a base for the missionaries (16:15). The first convert in Philippi was not a Jewish man, as elsewhere, but a Gentile woman.

The twists continued. Paul got into trouble not for his preaching, as in the past, but for a miracle. He drove a demon out of a slave girl. This enraged her owners because it ruined their prospects of continuing to profit from her predictions. They charged Paul and his companion Silas with promoting "un-Roman" customs and incited a crowd to attack them. Foregoing any investigation, city officials had Paul and Silas beaten with rods and thrown into prison (16:16–24). Paul later wrote to the Thessalonians that he and his companions had been "treated disgracefully" at Philippi (1 Thessalonians 2:2).

But Paul and Silas gave a twist of their own to this terrible situation. Instead of feeling sorry for themselves, they prayed and sang from the depths of their dungeon. Then God provided His unexpected twist in the form of an earthquake so violent that it opened all the locks that held the prisoners. The jailer, fearing a mass escape for which he would be held responsible, was about to commit suicide when Paul called out, "We are all here." The jailer went to Paul and Silas with the all-important question, "What is necessary for me to do in order that I might be saved?" (16:25–30).

The Greatest Twist

At just this dramatic moment, as the jailer received the answer to his question, we find the greatest twist. He was probably expecting a response such as, "Set us free," or a more religious answer, "Work to get on God's good side." The jailer was awaiting a command.

Any such answer requiring work would be in line with much thinking even today that says, "Do something so God will be pleased with you." We find this sort of advice all around us. It even creeps into the church.

But here is where the greatest twist occurs. Paul said, "Believe in the Lord Jesus and you will be saved, as well as your household" (16:31).

You may say that is a command. True, the grammatical form of Paul's statement was an imperative. But consider this: It is also a command, formally speaking, when someone hands food to a starving person and says, "Here, eat this." The individual understands that these words are actually an invitation. It does not enter the person's mind to complain and ask, "Who are you to order me around?"

The words Paul and Silas spoke to the Philippian jailer formed a life-giving invitation, not a directive to do work. While the jailer may have expected a command, in the great twist of justification by grace, what he received was a pure gift.

No doubt the jailer or his family would have recalled this blessing when, about 10 or 12 years after the earthquake, Paul wrote to the church at Philippi and said, "It has been *given* to you for Christ's sake not only to *believe* in Him but also to suffer for His sake" (Philippians 1:29, emphasis added). Faith is a gift, not a meritorious work. By God's grace, the jailer, a captor, became a captive of the Lord Jesus Christ on that special night—and his whole family with him (16:32–34). What a twist!

It is a twist we should hold high before the eyes of Christians. People sometimes think they have contributed to their salvation by determining to believe in Christ. Then they want to remain in the faith in the same way they think they entered it. Eventually they find they cannot. Their guilt mounts, and despair sets in.

God Himself keeps us sinners in the true faith (Philippians 1:6), just as He alone brings people to faith in the first place. He gives repentance and forgiveness of sins (5:31). That is a twist from the way you and I naturally think. But it helps to put aside any idea of conversion as a process to which we contribute and to say instead, "All glory be to God alone!"

The World Turned Upside Down

The second missionary journey was full of unexpected twists. It wasn't actually Paul and company who turned the world upside down (see 17:6), even when the apostle got an apology from the city officials at Philippi (16:35–40). The Lord was turning the world upside down, and the missionaries were along for the ride. As they discovered, His ways are not always our ways. But at every turn, He knew exactly what He was doing for the good of His church and for the expansion of His kingdom (Ephesians 1:22–23).

I once heard it said concerning Christ, "With the risen One, there is no such thing as a dead-end." Although at times Satan would like to have us believe otherwise, with our God at the helm, we can remain confident that with the risen Lord, there is no such thing as a dead-end. What a blessed assurance this is as we proceed day by day through life to eternal life with Him.

Chapter 16

Meet People Where They Are but Don't Leave Them There

Read Acts 17:1–18:22

It is an axiom of communication that a person with something to say should not talk over the heads of an audience. It is a good idea to "meet people where they are." But it is also important to help people grow, to take them beyond the place where one first finds them. I always have liked the addition someone made to the maxim, "… but don't leave them there." This is good wisdom for the church of every age, and it was certainly on the minds of Paul and his companions.

As we have seen, though, God's ways are not always our ways. The portion of the second missionary journey described in Acts 17 and 18 has its share of unexpected twists, as does Acts 16. Starting at Thessalonica, and continuing into Berea, Athens, and Corinth, the twists focused on meeting people where they were but not leaving them there. While this was no doubt Paul's intention, we also note that things did not always go according to his plans.

Thessalonica

At Thessalonica Paul resumed his practice of

teaching first in the synagogue. His message, as usual, was, "This is the Christ, this Jesus whom I proclaim to you." He backed it up with Old Testament Scripture. Paul's preaching had its effect, both among Jews and Gentiles, including "not a few of the leading women" (17:4).

However, Acts goes on to tell us that some of the Jews incited a crowd to cause a general uproar. Jason and others who befriended the missionaries were brought before local officials. While Jason and his friends managed to escape from that situation unharmed, the Christians took no chances with Paul and Silas. They hustled the two missionaries out of town for their protection (17:1–10).

But Paul remained deeply concerned about these new brothers and sisters in Christ whom he left behind. Acts notes that he had held forth in the synagogue at Thessalonica for three weeks—three sabbaths (17:2). Even if his overall stay in town lasted a bit longer than that, it was probably quite brief by any standard. Paul had tried to meet the Thessalonians where they were, but he was forced to leave before he could take them very far in what we might call catechetical instruction. He also knew that the fierce persecution that brought about his quick exit was going to attack the recently converted Christians of Thessalonica. Put together, these circumstances could have a disastrous impact.

Paul was rightly concerned. A solid foundation of Christian education combined with ongoing instruction in the faith is a must for us too. When I look at congregations and individual Christians across the country, and when I think about all the evil influences our world can exert, I understand why Paul carried such a burden for the folks back at Thessalonica. They had experienced only a few weeks' worth of Christian teaching.

It needs to be a top priority to study and teach the basics of the faith continuously. This process of instruction has come to be called "catechesis." Martin Luther wrote, "God Himself ... is not ashamed to teach the Christian doctrines every day. He knows of no better teachings than these; He always teaches these same ones; He presents nothing novel or different" (Janzow, p. 8; LC Preface 16). If God knows nothing better to teach, why should we have anything better to learn?

Later in the second missionary journey, during his time in Corinth, Paul was able to do a bit of "backfilling" by writing two letters to the Thessalonians. We get a real insight into the apostle's pastoral heart by reading these epistles. In the letters, Paul marveled at the power of God's Word that had brought his addressees to faith in Christ and kept them in it despite the adversity they had faced (1 Thessalonians 1:4–5; 2:13–14). Even so, he recognized there were "holes" remaining from his brief time of instruction among them. These "holes" required attention. For instance, they needed further guidance on sexual purity (1 Thessalonians 4:1–7) and the second coming of Christ (1 Thessalonians 4:13–5:11).

It is quite likely that, lacking background, the Thessalonians were not able to grasp adequately Paul's clarifications on the latter subject. His second epistle to the Thessalonians shows that some folks took Paul's words about Christ's second coming as an excuse to quit working and just wait for the Lord to come visibly (2 Thessalonians 3:6–15).

Anyone who doubts that doctrine affects living should make a careful study of 1 and 2 Thessalonians. For the sake of Christian faith and life, Paul wrote these epistles so he would not leave the Thessalonians where he first found them.

Berea

After being rushed out of Thessalonica, Paul and Silas moved on to Berea. Paul showed himself to be no more intimidated by the recent outbreak of trouble in Thessalonica than he had been by his earlier disgraceful treatment at Philippi. He and Silas went straight to the synagogue at Berea. There they encountered another unexpected twist—this time a most welcome one.

The Berean Jews turned out to be "more noble" than their counterparts at Thessalonica (17:11). They most willingly received the Word from these two missionaries for the Lord. But they were not gullible. "Daily they examined the Scriptures to see if these things were so" (17:11). The Scriptures provided the final standard by which they checked doctrine, even the Gospel proclamation brought by Paul. As before, Gentiles as well as Jews were converted, again including women of high standing (17:12).

Then came a chilling reminder of the days in Thessalonica. The Thessalonian Jews who opposed

Paul followed him to Berea! There they stirred up the crowds against him. Again, the apostle was forced to depart prematurely from a city. This time, however, he left Silas and Timothy behind to carry on.

Athens

Once more Paul, the itinerant missionary for Christ, found himself on the move. His next major stop was Athens (17:13–15). In his famous speech to the learned Greeks there, including many Epicurean and Stoic philosophers, Paul made a point to begin where they were. He had studied the city as well as the Scriptures.

Masking any disgust at the idolatry betokened by the array of statues and altars in Athens (17:16), Paul began with a straightforward observation: "I perceive that you are very religious." In fact, there was even an altar erected to an unknown god. Here was Paul's opening. He announced that he had come to proclaim the God they worshiped but did not know (17:22–23).

Remaining on common ground with the Athenians, Paul remarked that the true God does not live in man-made structures (17:24; compare 7:48). Instead, He gives life to all and is not far from anyone (17:25–27). Paul even quoted a couple Greek poets (17:28). The apostle did not hesitate to connect with the Athenians' natural knowledge of God.

So far the most startling thing in Paul's speech would have been his references to God in the singular. Next came the turning point in the address. While

God had overlooked the ignorance of the past, Paul said, now the time had arrived for everyone to repent. For this great God had set up a coming day in which judgment would be exercised by a Man of His choosing, as shown when He raised that Man from the dead (17:30–31). Paul was taking initial steps to lead his hearers carefully beyond the point where he first met them. He was far from finished, though. He had not yet mentioned the name "Jesus Christ."

But the speech was over. Paul hardly had rounded the bend in his address when he found that the great majority of his audience was no longer listening. The Athenians rejected the responsibility to God that Paul proclaimed. Even more, as good Greeks, they were convinced that the physical world was evil, so they dismissed out of hand any claim about a human body rising from the dead. Consequently, Acts reports that when Paul brought up the resurrection of Christ, some of his hearers started making fun of him. The more courteous among them gave him the equivalent of, "Don't call us; we'll call you" (17:32). His speech was over.

The Gospel was proving to be foolishness to Greeks as well as a stumbling block to Jews (1 Corinthians 1:23). But neither in his preaching to Jews nor to Greeks would Paul trim the message to the prevailing winds. How could he not speak of Christ's resurrection sooner or later? Paul simply had to take people further, beyond where he found them, to the One who is the power and wisdom of God (1 Corinthians 1:24).

We do too. At times I wonder, for example, about

some of the music we use in our task of catechesis. Many songs say little more than God is powerful, praiseworthy, or close by. And I ask with a shiver why we content ourselves to sing songs in which the scoffing Athenians could join also? Why are we not rounding the bend with St. Paul to sing of the God who reveals Himself in the Christ who died for our sins and on the third day was raised again for our justification? Only in Him, and on account of His work, do we have a gracious and forgiving God.

Corinth

Paul's last stop on the second missionary journey proved to be the site where he remained the longest—Corinth. A vital seaport on an isthmus through which sea commerce passed between east and west, Corinth was capital of the Roman province of southern Greece. Here Paul lived with a Jewish Christian couple, Aquila and Priscilla, and engaged in the tent-making trade (18:1–3).

Early in his 18-month stay at Corinth, Paul and the message of Christ were rejected at the synagogue (18:5–6)—although the synagogue ruler and his household were converted. Paul finally ended up preaching at a location next to the synagogue (18:7–8). But the future of the church in Corinth lay with the Gentiles.

In many ways this was not a comforting prospect for Paul. If the apostle was still scratching his head over his experience in Athens, what he saw in front of him at Corinth was downright daunting. In Corinth, as at Athens, temples to idols were plentiful. Even worse, the city was celebrated for its decadence. Prostitution was rampant. People all over the Mediterranean world knew what it meant to "sin like a Corinthian."

Paul may have been wondering how to meet *these* people where they were when the Lord appeared to him and said, "Stop being afraid. Rather, speak and do not be silent. I am with you." In time, Paul learned the truth of Jesus' closing words, "I have many people in this city" (18:9–10). Another unexpected twist!

Acts also records that the Jews hauled Paul before the Roman provincial governor, Gallio, on charges resembling those the Sanhedrin had given to Pontius Pilate concerning Jesus (John 19:7). But before Paul could make a defense, Gallio dismissed the case as a Jewish matter to be settled internally (18:12–17). Jesus had been executed by the order of a Roman governor, but throughout the history of the early church as told in Acts, no Christian was found guilty of anything by a Roman. That too is an unexpected twist.

Meet people where they are, but do not leave them there. I believe this is one of the most challenging things a pastor or any Christian can do. In my travels, I have often heard both professional church workers and laypeople echoing this sentiment. While it is not the easiest task in the world, the Lord places this challenge before us. And He gives us the firm promise of His blessing through His powerful Gospel.

Even if benign Romans such as Gallio were content to leave Christianity right where they found it, through the work of men such as Paul the ascended Lord was still teaching, still doing His saving work through His Word in countless lives to the ends of the earth. Today, Christ guides the church's every effort to meet people where they are with the grace of God and then to move them on from that place. With that in mind, we can take whatever unexpected twists He sees fit to send us.

Section H

Pay Attention to Common Human Experiences

As we traveled from one location to the next in our travel trailer, we met many people. When you park in your campsite, there are families on either side of you, behind you, and across the road from you. The door of opportunity stands wide open for you to observe and meet your temporary neighbors.

In a way, you find more friendly and outgoing people in a campground than you do in a motel. Often the children break the ice. They visit with one another, and soon their parents do the same. The men discuss motor homes and gas prices, and the women discuss their families or their destinations.

As this happens, one cannot help noticing that certain traits are shared by everyone, whether city dwellers, small-town natives, or those from rural settings. Everyone laughs. Everyone gets frustrated. Everyone gets angry or enjoys a good joke. Everyone has hopes and fears. There is a commonality of emotion that seems to run through the whole human race.

In a way, this fact helps us identify with the feelings and reactions of those we meet. It also helps us identify their strengths and weaknesses.

In our trip through Acts, I would like to suggest that you *pay attention to common human experiences.* Wherever and whenever people are involved—even on the pages of Scripture—human characteristics, emotions, temptations, and sins come into play. We are intimately acquainted with these things. We feel their impact. We can use this familiarity to help us grasp the ways human experiences affected the people about whom we read.

In the case of Scripture, God committed His Word to writing through people for the sake of people. He does not hesitate to speak through the language of common experience. In this section of our journey, we find Paul confronting two powerful aspects of human emotion—anger and warm personal affection. Special blessings, as we look at these common human traits and how they play into our ongoing lives in Christ.

Chapter 17

Anger and Opposition

Read Acts 18:23–19:41

In this sinful world, one of the most powerful and most unpleasant aspects of common human experience is anger. It sets people against one another. It derails rational consideration of any matter at hand. It can be especially dangerous in a group, spreading like wildfire and perhaps erupting in terrible violence. Everyone knows what anger can do. Acts 19 connects with the reader's knowledge of anger to suggest the obstacles Paul faced on his third missionary journey.

The account of this missionary journey does not open with the attention-getting features that marked the stories of Paul's earlier trips (13:1–4; 15:36–41). We find no details about the circumstances under which he departed or the personnel he took along. There is little or nothing in the text to indicate the start of a major expedition. In very matter-of-fact language, Acts 18:23 says Paul set out for some of the cities he had visited on his first journey. This simple statement relates the start and early stages of Paul's most ambitious missionary journey to date.

Ephesus

It is as if Luke could not wait to write about Ephesus. That city, at the time the fourth largest in the Roman Empire, was Paul's major objective on this trip. During his second journey, he had not reached it during the early going (16:6). And he stopped there only briefly at the end to drop off Priscilla and Aquila (18:19–21). Paul's work at Ephesus formed the heart of his third journey, both as to time spent there (three years) and the space devoted to it in Acts.

Easily the metropolis of western Asia Minor, Ephesus was a provincial capital like Corinth. Also like Corinth, it was a port city and a center of commerce. It saw its share of immorality. Like all Gentile cities, Ephesus was a hotbed of idolatry. Its temple to the Greek goddess Artemis found a place among the fabled seven wonders of the ancient world. But for some reason, Ephesus also exerted an unusually strong attraction for magicians, soothsayers, and superstitious folk of many stripes. Documents containing spells and bits of sorcery often were called "Ephesian writings."

Eager to proclaim the Gospel in this environment, Paul stayed longer in Ephesus than in any other city. Of course everyone there needed the Savior, but the impact of the mission also had every potential to reverberate well beyond that city, and Paul knew it.

The apostle was carrying out an aggressive plan of outreach. In a way, his approach resembles the strategy of a hard-nosed football coach who tells players to attack their opponents' strength rather than nibbling away at the other team's weaknesses. If the church gained a foothold in a major pagan center like Ephesus, great things could happen all over Asia Minor.

Don't Stay with the Easy Stuff

We would do well to ponder this missionary approach. Much of the evangelistic literature aimed at U.S. churches provides strong encouragement to concentrate on reaching out to people who appear to be comparatively "easy prospects." In effect, the message seems to be that Christians shouldn't waste their efforts elsewhere.

This advice is questionable. First, from the womb all people are equally dead in trespasses and sins (Ephesians 2:1). Therefore, no one is truly an "easier" prospect than another. Second, if we think in terms of those we find it easiest to relate to socially, we certainly can develop a list of prospects. It can prove tempting to concentrate on this list to the exclusion of other people. But Paul's example at Ephesus reminds us that we should not neglect bringing the Gospel to the places and people we consider difficult.

Often, these groups of people seem difficult because they aren't "like us." They may be intellectuals at universities or mentally disabled. They could be members of a different ethnic group. They may be adherents of non-Christian religions such as Islam, Judaism, or Hinduism or of cults like the Mormons or Jehovah's Witnesses. Such outreach may require the investment of extra planning and effort so we can be better prepared to speak of Christ with members of these groups.

In any case, let's not neglect the "tough" prospect. Frequently, this means we simply have to move off dead center and start. What would have happened if

Paul had decided to skip Ephesus because the going probably would be too rough?

Rough Going

Paul's going *was* rough in Ephesus. He later spoke of the trials he experienced there "through the plots of the Jews" (20:19). He told the Corinthians that, humanly speaking, he fought with wild beasts at Ephesus (1 Corinthians 15:32). Those are frightening words, even if Paul meant them figuratively. He wrote from Ephesus that an important door was open to him and that there were "many adversaries" (1 Corinthians 16:9).

Later, Paul recalled a time when he and his companions at Ephesus despaired of life itself. But this sense of hopelessness helped return them to dependence on "the God who raises the dead" (2 Corinthians 1:8–9). The mission remained the Lord's and they remained the Lord's, even in tough situations like those they faced at Ephesus. And today the God and Father of our Lord Jesus Christ—the God who raises the dead—has lost none of His power to create new life in those to whom we speak the Gospel. He is equally able to take care of us now and forever.

In his epistles, Paul vividly described his rough going in Ephesus. But what about the account in Acts of Paul's Ephesian ministry? Does it say anything along these lines?

Acts Describes Paul's Work in Ephesus

Acts indicates that Paul's preaching in Ephesus

began typically enough. First, he held forth in the synagogue. Then he left because of the unbelief and slander he encountered there. He ended up at a lecture hall. It seems to have been available during the middle of the day when no other activities would have been scheduled because of the heat. Although this may not have been Paul's most comfortable classroom, it turned out to be a popular one. There, he taught the Lord's Word to both Jews and Gentiles for two years (19:8–11).

The Lord used Paul to work amazing miracles (19:11–12) that caught the eye of traveling Jewish exorcists. We already have called attention to the lesson the sons of Sceva learned the hard way. Jesus' name was far more than a mere "handle" and certainly not a magic formula. When these unbelievers treated it as such, a demon-possessed man attacked them and overpowered them (19:13–16).

News of this event went out on the grapevine among the sorcerers and magicians in Ephesus. It caused even more attention to be focused on the Jesus preached by Paul. At first, "fear fell on them all," then "the name of the Lord Jesus was held in high honor" (19:17).

One thing led to another. There was public confession by some of Paul's Ephesian converts who had not totally broken with their old pagan practices. Even more people still mired in magic staged a huge book-burning of their various occult texts. The monetary value of these "Ephesian writings" approximated the amount that an average laborer would be paid for about 50,000 days of work—and it all went up in smoke! The Word of the Lord had won a stunning victory in Ephesus (19:18–20).

The Riot

While Acts shows the triumph of the Gospel at Ephesus, it does not omit the rough going Paul and other Christians faced. One anecdote, packed with explosive anger, says it all. We can readily picture the scene. And we are awestruck at the potential for violence, just as we might gasp at Paul's phrase about the wild beasts he faced at Ephesus. What the devil loses in one way, he tries to make up for in others.

Demetrius, a silversmith, made a speech in which he appealed to his fellow craftsmen's profession, their wallets, their sense of civic pride, and their religiosity. Without sales of the small silver shrines he and the others made, Demetrius contended, the great temple of Artemis at Ephesus would lose prestige. This blow to the temple's reputation could extend to the goddess herself, he continued. Demetrius added there was a culprit actively at work to bring about such ruin for Ephesus—Paul, who had been saying far and wide that gods made with hands are not really gods at all (19:23–27).

The silversmiths' anger flared. "Great is Artemis of the Ephesians!" came their cry (19:28). Moving across town to the amphitheater, they aroused others as they went. They also grabbed two of Paul's colleagues and dragged them along. "The city was filled with confusion" (19:29).

Paul wanted to enter the fray, perhaps to try to

calm things down, but his friends advised him not to go (19:30–31). Their wisdom was borne out by the treatment given to someone named Alexander, who tried to address the crowd on behalf of the Jewish community. Nobody listened to him (19:33–34). Things easily could have grown worse.

The elements of a classic mob scene were in place. Some people cried one thing, some another. Most did not know why they were there in the first place. The crowd took on a will of its own. For two hours it continued the cheer, "Great is Artemis of the Ephesians!" (19:32, 34). Finally, a city official managed to restore order. He advised anyone who had a grievance to pursue it lawfully. Then he told everyone to go home (19:35–41). The mob scene ended almost as quickly as it had begun.

Anger and Opposition Today

Facing opposition for Christ's sake has never been fun. It would be so much more enjoyable if our travel could always be calm and peaceful. But that is not the way life is, especially for Christians. The world that hated our Lord will hate us too (John 15:18).

It is never easy to bear the world's anger and hatred, but facing opposition can be helpful too. It can help us remain focused on the truly important issues of faith and life and prevent us from becoming too accustomed to this world. The God who raises the dead remains with us.

Of all people, it hardly would have surprised the Christians at Ephesus to read in Paul's later epistle that "our struggle is not against flesh and blood, but against rulers … [and] authorities" in the supernatural realm. Against these, Paul said, put on the armor of God. And we should not forget the weapon Paul always used on the offensive: the sword of the Spirit, God's Word (Ephesians 6:12–17).

As one who knew what anger can do, Paul also wrote, "Be angry but do not sin" (Ephesians 4:26). Drawing attention not only to the pattern but also to the power the Lord provides, the apostle proclaimed a better way: "Walk in love, just as Christ also loved us and gave Himself for us, a sweet-smelling offering and sacrifice to God" (Ephesians 5:2).

Many in Ephesus took Paul's message to heart during his three-year stay. They were bound with him in Christ by strong bonds of love. That will be the leading story in the next chapter.

Chapter 18

Love and Support

Read Acts 20

We continue to *pay attention to common human experiences* as we read the narrative of Acts. In the last chapter, we saw anger and its destructive forces rear their ugly heads in Ephesus. This time we have a beautiful instance of love and support. As before, our familiarity with such elements of common human experience serves us well as we read.

Acts briefly touches on Paul's itinerary after the riot at Ephesus: He traveled into Macedonia and Greece, then back through Macedonia (20:1–3). In only somewhat greater detail, Acts recounts the story of Eutychus, a young man who fell asleep during a sermon. I won't comment on how long the sermon was (20:7–12).

Much of Paul's activity on this leg of his third missionary journey went unrecorded by Luke. No mention is made of the epistle to the Romans, which Paul probably wrote during his three-month stay in Greece. As we saw at the start of the third missionary journey (18:23), the narrative moves rapidly through the first half of Acts 20. In this it resembles Paul, who was rushing to get to Jerusalem in time for Pentecost (20:13–16).

A Return to Ephesus

At this point in Acts, Luke was inspired by God to pause in the midst of a fast-paced report to record one more episode involving the church at Ephesus. Paul did not want to go to Ephesus itself, thinking that such a side trip might disrupt his travel plans. Instead, he sent for the elders, or pastors, from Ephesus and told them to meet him at Miletus. In the second half of Acts 20, we read Paul's farewell address to these beloved brothers and co-workers with whom he had lived and worked for three years. It is a moving scene, reflecting mutual love and support.

When he first became acquainted with these men, they were new converts to Christ. As time went by, they were among the faithful laypeople to whom he preached at Ephesus. He knew them well, and he loved them. Recalling my years of parish ministry, I can remember one layperson after another whose lives and words were such a joy to me in the Lord.

As Paul made his farewell address, he was looking at familiar and beloved faces. These, in turn, probably reminded him of still other cherished people at Ephesus or in other cities where he had proclaimed the Gospel.

Faithfulness from the First Day

With a full heart, Paul began his message, "You yourselves know how I lived with you the whole time from the first day I came into the province of Asia. I acted as a slave for the Lord with all humility, with tears, and in trials which came about for me via the plots of the Jews" (20:18–19). As we already have seen, things had not been easy for Paul at Ephesus.

But Paul stuck it out. "I shrank back neither from telling you things that would help you nor from teaching you publicly and from house to house. Rather, I declared solemnly and emphatically, both to Jews and Greeks, repentance toward God and faith in our Lord Jesus" (20:20–21). Paul loved the Lord and he loved people too much to spin his wheels or to try to tell audiences only what they wanted to hear. Proclaiming the message of sin and grace was too urgent, too important a priority, to be dismayed by peril or derailed by pride.

The same should hold true today. A pastor has to preach God's Word no matter the time, place, or situation in which he finds himself. He is called to speak the Word to the churched and the unchurched, from the pulpit, at the hospital bed, in the classroom, at home, to young as well as old and those in-between. This is a great delight and privilege in the Lord. And what a blessing it is for a congregation to have a faithful pastor!

Expendable for the Kingdom

"And now, you see, I am going to Jerusalem, bound in the Spirit, not knowing what will happen to me there," Paul continued, "except that the Holy Spirit tells me that chains and troubles await me in every town" (20:22–23). Paul was not paralyzed by the prospect of troubles or even of chains. He had learned, as Christians always have to learn and relearn, that in Christ we already have died. It is Christ who lives in us (Galatians 2:20).

Thus, Paul told the Ephesian elders, "By no means do I reckon my life as worth anything. The important thing is to complete my course and the ministry which I received from the Lord Jesus, emphatically to declare the Gospel of the grace of God" (20:24). Paul knew he was expendable for the sake of the kingdom. This remains the way of love and the way of Christ.

Paul continued, "And now I know that none of you, among whom I went around preaching the kingdom, will see my face again. Therefore, I testify to you on this very day that I am innocent of the blood of you all, for I did not shrink back from telling you the whole plan of God" (20:25–27). A pastor always must take full advantage of the opportunities the Lord grants him to teach and exhort. God's people need to be thoroughly grounded in the Word of life, not just acquainted with its high points or the parts we find agreeable.

The old Adam in each of us does not want to hear anything our God has to say, whether curse or blessing. The Lord sends pastors to His church, to oppose the sinful flesh, especially so the Good News will be repeated again and again to comfort and save us.

Watch Out for the Flock

God sends pastors to His church for the sake of the Gospel. Knowing this, Paul went on, "Watch out for yourselves and the whole flock among whom the Holy Spirit has made you overseers [or *bishops*]" (20:28a; compare 20:24). Rest assured that God Himself has sent your congregation every one of its pastors. Even though pastors are sinners placed into office by sinners who work through call processes tainted by sin, the Holy Spirit Himself works through it all. He made these men pastors (shepherds) of the sheep and overseers of the flock. To attack or ignore a pastor sent by God who is faithfully proclaiming God's message is to disregard the Holy Spirit's leading in the ongoing life of the congregation. To receive in repentance and faith the message spoken by God's faithful messenger is in a way a return to baptism, where our sins are washed away in Christ.

It is true that the Lord sent pastors for His church, and He still does, for the sake of the Gospel. Their work, as Paul put it, was "to shepherd the church of God which He acquired through His own blood" (20:28b). Pastors serve as undershepherds of the great Shepherd, who laid down His life for the sheep and took it up again (John 10:11–18), the One brought again from the dead by God (Hebrews 13:20ff). Pastors point not to themselves, but to Christ—to His cross and empty tomb, His Word and sacraments.

It is a great shame and sin when someone produces turmoil in God's provision to feed His sheep good spiritual food through His servants, His ministers. That, of course, is exactly what the devil wants to do. Therefore, Paul told the pastors from Ephesus, "I am well aware that after I leave, fierce wolves will come in among you, not sparing the flock ... men from among you will get up and say distorted things to draw away disciples after themselves. Therefore be alert, remembering that for three years, day and night, I did not cease instructing each one of you with tears" (20:29–31). Paul did not hesitate to do this labor of love. His work was a matter of life and death—or rather, a matter of death and life on account of the crucified and risen Christ.

Entrusted to God

It is hard to leave those one has grown to love to face an uncertain and even dangerous future. Here is how Paul did it: "And now I entrust you to God and to the Word of His grace, which is able to build you up and give you the inheritance which goes to all who are sanctified" (20:32).

God builds His church through His means of grace. When I was a parish pastor, I was aware that people did not return to church week after week to hear me or to find out what new theory I had cooked up. They came to hear the Word of the Lord Jesus Christ.

Through the Word, the Master Himself admonishes the erring, forgives the sinner, comforts the fainthearted, supports the suffering, and wipes away tears from their eyes. He did these things in every congregation I served long before I arrived, and He continued to do them while I was privileged to serve in that place. When the time came for me to leave, I could rest assured that He would continue to do them. I could leave with an upbeat attitude about the future because I was confident in the One who holds the future in His hand.

Paul had reached a climactic point in his address as he committed his hearers—and their hearers—to God and His Word. One *commits* or *entrusts* something because it is valuable (14:23; see Luke 23:46 and 2 Timothy 1:12). The church certainly is valuable, bought with the blood of God Himself in Jesus Christ (20:28).

Because Paul knew that he was valuable to God, he could continue, "I did not covet anyone's silver, gold, or clothing. You know that my hands served my needs and those of my companions. In every way I showed you that it is necessary for us, by this kind of hard work, to come to the help of the weak and to remember the words that the Lord Jesus Himself said: 'It is more blessed to give than to receive' " (20:33–35).

The apostle who freely had received so much from God was able freely to give to others. This also is the way of love and the way of Christ.

Bonds of Love

At the end of Paul's farewell address, he joined the Ephesian pastors on their knees for prayer. A tender and touching time ensued. Everyone wept, embracing Paul and kissing him (20:36–38). What a bond of love! What a tremendous example of mutual support! I am certain Paul and his Ephesian co-workers recalled this day often.

As I read these words and reflect on the bonds of love and mutual support that I have seen between countless pastors and congregations, I can only say, "Thanks, God, for the spirit of love, self-sacrifice, and boldness You have given our pastors. And thank You for the laypeople who hear Your good Word and stand on it together with their pastors. Please, God, daily draw us closer together as You draw us closer to Yourself in Jesus Christ."

As for Paul, he had work to do that would take him farther westward than he had been before. The surprise would be the way he got there. That's the subject of the last section.

Section I

Pay Attention to Action Described in Detail

By now you have gathered that our whole family liked not only to take trips in our travel trailer but also to recall and discuss what we had seen and done. If all my stories have not yet made it clear, I like to talk about our trips too, even after all these years.

When we, as a family, start talking about our vacations, it's fairly easy to tell what we consider the most memorable or the most important part of each trip. You just need to time the conversation. The things we spend the most time discussing are undoubtedly the things that stood out the most. I suspect you and your family operate the same way.

In this final section of our journey together in Acts, we turn our attention to one last idea that can help us read narrative: *pay attention to action described in detail*. This is good advice, even for listening to vacation reminiscences. But it is especially pertinent for reading the Bible, as well as other ancient literature. Because writing materials were rather expensive in the ancient world and it required additional time and money to make extra copies, any ancient writer who devoted page after page to an event presumably regarded it as quite weighty.

Again we recall that God is the ultimate author of Scripture. This is something we can never forget. In his comments on Genesis, Martin Luther once remarked, "I myself wonder why Moses has so much to say about such unimportant matters when above he has been very concise in matters far more sublime. There is no doubt, however, that the Holy Spirit wanted these things to be written and to stand for our instruction; for in Holy Scripture nothing unimportant is put before us, and nothing unprofitable" (LW vol. 4, 274). When the Lord describes something in detail, it stands out as worthy of our attention.

Of all the events recorded in Acts, the description of Paul's trip to Rome was laid out in the greatest detail. It forms the subject for the last two chapters.

Chapter 19

A Period of Trials

Read Acts 21–26

Paul's voyage to Rome is described in great detail in Acts. In fact, we already see details of the trip during the account of his third missionary journey. While still in Ephesus, Paul announced that his travel plans were to go first to Jerusalem and then to the capital city of the Roman Empire. Even before the riot at Ephesus, the apostle had said, "It is necessary for me also to see Rome" (19:21; compare Luke 9:51). Note that Paul used the same expression ("it is necessary") that Jesus used to refer to His messianic work (Luke 9:22; Luke 17:25; Luke 24:26). This was also the term the ascended Lord used when speaking to Ananias about Paul. "I will show him what *it is necessary* for him to suffer for the sake of My name" (9:16, emphasis added).

The last portion of Acts is filled with parallels between Christ and Paul. For example, both appeared before the Sanhedrin (the Jewish council, 23:1–10; Luke 22:66–71), a Roman governor (24:1–21; Luke 23:1ff), and a Herodian king (26:1–32; Luke 23:7–11). Like the Master, Paul wanted God's will to be done above all else (21:13–14; Luke 22:42). In a real sense, Paul was following in Jesus' footsteps as the Lord used him to distribute the blessings of salvation by bringing the Gospel beyond Jerusalem to Rome (Colossians 1:24–29).

The Unique Last Quarter of Acts

Paul's voyage to Rome emerges as the central concern of Luke's inspired account as the narrative of the third missionary journey ends in Acts 21. From Acts 21 to Acts 28, the story of the trip to Rome unfolds in detail. Most of the description is devoted to a period of trials.

This last quarter of Acts is unique. Here the spotlight focuses on Paul and the legal proceedings in which he was embroiled. In Acts 21–28, we find the apostle starting no new churches and visiting no established ones, except those in Jerusalem and Rome. There were hardly any conversions to report. Paul's progress to Rome must have been momentous to merit such detailed coverage.

Rumblings of Trouble

The trip did not start on a pleasant note. At Tyre and Caesarea, Paul was warned that trouble awaited him in Jerusalem (21:4, 10–11). For that matter, Paul himself seems to have anticipated difficulties when he wrote to the Roman church asking for prayers that he be delivered from unbelievers in Judea (Romans 15:31).

But Paul remained steadfast about going to Jerusalem. He was determined to present the offering that he had gathered for the relief of the Christians there. In the epistle to the Romans, Paul also had requested them to pray "that my service for Jerusalem may be acceptable to the saints" (Romans 15:31; see Romans 15:25–27).

As he wrote these words, Paul was cherishing the hope that after a stop in Jerusalem he would be free to go to Rome. Eventually, of course, his freedom became a casualty of the arrest and trials described in Acts 21–26. Through it all, though, the Lord assured Paul that he eventually would make it to Rome (23:11; 27:24).

Trouble Breaks Out

Upon Paul's arrival in Jerusalem, James suggested a plan for the apostle to the Gentiles to show that he had not grown ashamed of his Jewish roots (21:17–24). It called for Paul to participate in a week-long temple ritual, but before the week ended, Paul had been seized by a mob that had been stirred up by "Jews from Asia" (21:27).

Paul likely would have been stoned if the Roman soldiers at nearby Tower Antonia had not intervened. While in their custody, Paul told his story to the crowd. Here we find Paul's conversion recounted for the second time in Acts (22:1–21). But during the speech, the mob again exploded in anger, forcing the Romans to take Paul away from the scene (22:22–24).

On Trial for the Resurrection

The next day, Paul told the Sanhedrin, "I am being judged concerning the hope and the resurrection of the dead" (23:6). At these words the Pharisees, who believed in the general resurrection, started disputing with the Sadducees, who denied it (23:7–8). This turned out to be a potent legal defense tactic, rendering the council unable to give the Romans a sensible reason to hold Paul.

But Paul's words were not just a ploy to start an argument. As he had defended himself in other settings, Paul reasserted that he was on trial concerning the "resurrection of the dead" (24:21; see 24:15 and 26:8) and the ancient "hope" of Israel (26:6–7; see 24:15 and 28:20). We may think it would have been easier for Paul to say that he was in legal trouble because of "Christ" (as he did in Philippians 1:13), but to him all three expressions meant the same thing.

Paul kept saying that Christ was the fulfillment of the promise in which Israel's hope rested. "To this day I stand bearing witness both to small and great, saying nothing outside of what the prophets and Moses predicted, that the Christ must suffer and, as the *first among the resurrection of the dead*, He would proclaim light both to the people and to the Gentiles," Paul proclaimed (26:22–23, emphasis added). Paul never forgot that not only had Christ Himself risen, but He also became the first of all the dead to rise. To talk about Christ *is* to talk about the resurrection.

Paul was saying the same thing the other apostles had said during the early days in Jerusalem when they "proclaimed in Jesus the resurrection of the dead" (4:2). While the Pharisees and other first-century Jews may have thought of the resurrection as an abstract idea, Christians knew it was as real as the new life of their risen Lord. In the living Christ are refreshment and restoration (3:20–21). He is the "first-fruits of those who sleep" (1 Corinthians 15:20; see Colossians 1:18). No wonder Acts simply character-izes the subject of Paul's preaching at Athens as "Jesus and the resurrection" (17:18).

I know a man who is fond of saying that Jesus Christ is "Mister Resurrection." If you think about one, the other springs to mind almost automatically. When we ponder Christ's resurrection, we are reminded of our resurrection and deliverance from the trials we have in this world. Martin Luther said:

> The resurrection is to be viewed and under-stood as having already begun in Christ, indeed, as being more than half finished … For the main and best part of this has already come to pass, namely, that Christ, our Head, has arisen … For where the head goes and abides, there the body with all the members must necessarily follow and abide. (*LW vol. 28, p. 110*)

Luther made this point personal for every Chris-tian by adding, "In short, our head, yes, our back and our belly, our shoulders and legs have already passed from death, and all the hold death still has on us is by a small toe. This, too, will extricate itself soon" (LW vol. 28, p. 120). While we saw hints of this relation-ship between Jesus' resurrection and ours in previous sections of Acts—for example, it was the essence of every baptism that Luke reported—not until Paul's speeches of self-defense en route to Rome did this comforting truth appear in full view.

Perils and Defenses

After Paul appeared before the Sanhedrin, a plot to kill him was discovered (23:12–22). For his protection, the Roman military moved him by night from detention in Jerusalem to Caesarea, where governor Felix would hear his case (23:23–35). The high priest and elders came from Jerusalem to lodge their complaints (24:1). Quoting their words, Luther observed that "anyone who wants to proclaim Christ and to confess that He is our righteousness will immediately be forced to hear that he is a 'persistent fellow' (Acts 24:5) who is stirring up everything" (LW vol. 26, p. 451–452).

Again Paul defended himself by, among other things, noting that the Jews from Asia who had stirred up the mob in Jerusalem had not come to make an accusation against him (24:18–19). Here the apostle had Roman law on his side.

The trial might have ended at this point, just a few days after it started. But Felix dragged his heels about rendering a decision, even though he was acquainted with the Christian movement (24:22). It seems the corrupt governor did not want to aggravate the Jews by releasing Paul—unless the prisoner could make it worth his while by offering a bribe (24:26–27). So Felix allowed Paul to languish in minimum security confinement at Caesarea for the next two years (24:23, 27).

Felix's replacement, Porcius Festus, determined to expedite Paul's case. As a new governor, he no doubt wanted to get off to a good start with the

Jerusalem authorities. Wanting to do them a favor, he suggested that Paul be tried in Jerusalem (25:9). Unwittingly, though, Festus was aiding and abetting a plot that already had been hatched to assassinate Paul (25:3). It was then that Paul used his prerogative as a Roman citizen to appeal to Caesar (25:10–11).

To Rome as a Prisoner

For two years, Paul probably had wondered when and how the Lord would keep His promise to get him to Rome (23:11). Now it all became clear: Paul would go to Rome as a prisoner awaiting trial rather than go to Jerusalem where certain death was waiting. Again, the Romans became Paul's protectors from Jews who rejected the Gospel of justification by grace.

Paul's appearance before Festus, together with King Herod Agrippa II and his sister Bernice, was an anticlimax as far as the legal trial was concerned. The extradition decision already had been made (25:13–22). But this elaborately described occasion was important because it afforded Paul another opportunity to tell the story of his conversion in the presence of high officials. This is the third and final time the conversion story is told in Acts (26:2–23). This also is the last lengthy speech by Paul recorded in Acts.

Privately, Agrippa told Festus that Paul could have been released if he had not appealed to Caesar (26:32). But matters were now out of their hands in a manner more profound than they could have dreamed. The Lord was taking Paul to Rome. Even as Christ Himself had undergone multiple legal processes and trials on His way to the cross, Paul was going to endure trials at the heart of the empire for Jesus' sake.

It is no accident that we find the greatest emphasis on the Christian's victory in Christ's resurrection at just the spot in Acts where Paul's trials are described in the greatest detail. The sure hope of his resurrection and life in glory with Christ enabled the apostle to go on. And it is the same for us.

While I was a parish pastor, and since then as well, I have shared the resurrection hope in Christ with many people who had lost a loved one in death or who were facing death themselves. I believe nothing draws a pastor and his people closer than the loss of loved ones. While sorrow is evident among the survivors, faith and hope in the risen Lord come to the forefront during this hour of trial. Repeatedly I have heard people remark that they did not know what they would have done had it not been for their victorious Lord and His promises. How true!

I have noted that Christians are sometimes cautioned not to be so heavenly minded that they are of "no earthly good." While I understand the point behind this phrase, I think it is far better to identify the heavenly minded Christian as exactly the one who can do the most good here and now. When we set our minds on the things that are above (Colossians 3:1–4), we have a clarity of vision and a depth of courage from our God that enables us to get significantly involved in the truly consequential things of this life. Because of the resurrection—Christ's and ours—we are assured that our labor for the Lord is never in vain (1 Corinthians 15:58).

Chapter 20

To the Ends of the Earth

Read Acts 27–28

In the previous chapter, we emphasized the need to *pay attention to action described in detail.* In the present chapter, we again employ this wisdom as we read how Acts concludes with Paul's voyage to Rome.

Without a doubt, this qualifies as a detailed account. Acts 27 has been admired by nautical historians for its vivid and careful reporting of an excursion, a storm, and a shipwreck. Paul and those with him would make it to Rome but not without going through some pretty harrowing events.

A Bad Time to Travel

The crew and passengers knew they were sailing late in the season. It was probably sometime in October because the Day of Atonement had passed (27:9). On November 10, the Romans considered the Mediterranean closed for the winter for shipping. The sea would become increasingly dangerous with each passing day.

The voyage began at Caesarea. After hugging the

Palestinian coastline up to Sidon, the ship set out against the prevailing winds as far as Myra, a city on the southern coast of Asia Minor. There the centurion who was guarding Paul booked passage for them on an Alexandrian grain ship bound for Italy. If anything could get them through unfavorable waters, a large freighter like this seemed to offer the best prospect (27:1–6).

But weather conditions worsened. They made it with difficulty through the open sea to a location called Fair Havens on the south side of the island of Crete. But the captain, the ship's owner (who happened to be aboard), and the Roman centurion decided that those havens were not fair enough to spend the winter. Against Paul's advice, they decided to make a last-ditch effort to reach the harbor at Phoenix, farther west on Crete (27:7–12).

The Storm

At first, things went well. But soon a northeaster, a storm with hurricane-force winds, enveloped them. For two weeks the ship was tossed about, unable to navigate because neither sun nor stars were visible from the heart of the storm. Ballast was thrown overboard to offer the best chance of staying afloat, but despair set in, even among the grizzled veterans of the sea (27:13–20, 27).

As Acts 27 unfolds, the Lord's hand becomes more and more prominent. No one else could take care of Paul and the others. God was the only one who could keep the promise that Paul would eventually stand before Caesar. As we know, His strength is made perfect in human weakness (2 Corinthians 12:9). The apostle announced to the ship's company that through an angelic visit, he knew no one would die (27:21–26). When Paul later cautioned against trying to escape in a lifeboat (27:27–32) and then encouraged the 276 aboard to eat something (27:33–38), his words were heeded.

The Shipwreck

Finally, the ship ran aground on shoals off Malta. After being spared from the storm, Paul might have been killed by Roman soldiers as they initiated a standard practice of putting their prisoners to the sword when escape was a possibility. But the centurion prevented this (27:39–44).

Ashore on Malta, trying to warm himself after the shipwreck, Paul was gathering firewood when a viper bit him. He was as good as dead then, too, but thanks again to the Lord's protection, Paul miraculously survived (28:1–6). Over and over again, the Master showed Himself to be completely serious about His promise that Paul would bear witness to Him in Rome (23:11).

Rome

When Paul reached the great city in the spring, the apostle probably had to pinch himself. It had been a long time since the mob had seized him at Jerusalem (21:30). At that time it looked as though he would never travel this far west. It had been longer still since

Paul had first announced his resolution in the Spirit to see Rome (19:21). In gratitude to God, Paul took courage when he saw the Roman Christians who came to greet him (28:15). He had written to these people about his evangelistic plans and dreams (Romans 15:22–24, 28–29). Now he was finally meeting them face to face.

To the Jew First

Upon his arrival, Paul set about following a familiar pattern. He spoke with the Jews of Rome, summarizing how he had come to wear his chains (28:17–20). He found the Jewish population unprejudiced regarding his case, although they had heard negative rumors about Christianity (28:21–22).

Because of Paul's house arrest, the Jews had to come to him. Many did come to hear him on an appointed day (28:16–17, 23). As usual, Paul proclaimed Christ and the kingdom of God from the Old Testament, and as usual reactions were mixed (28:23–24; see Luke 2:34–35).

Before the unbelieving Jews left for home, though, Paul had a parting word for them from the prophet Isaiah (Isaiah 6:9–10). This quote, often repeated in the New Testament (Luke 8:9–10 and parallels; John 12:39–40), shows God's response to human unbelief. Those who do not hear will not hear. This happened in Israel all the way back to the time of the prophets. And it was still happening now that the Messiah had come, although many individual Jews like Paul himself had become Christians.

The apostle's final words to the Jews were: "Let it be known to you that this salvation of God has been sent out to the Gentiles. They will listen" (28:28). We previously have encountered this theme in Acts (13:46–47 and 18:6) as the church steadily became more populated by Gentiles and less by Jews. Here was perhaps the most pointed statement yet. As we reflect on it, we should bear three things in mind.

First, we have learned from Scripture not to think that Paul had somehow grown to hate his ancestral people, the Jews. He was very careful to say that while he had received unjust treatment at the hands of some Jews, he had no charge to bring against his people (28:19; see 24:17). Paul had written that he himself would rather be cut off from Christ than to see the Jews perish (Romans 9:1–5). Paul had not spent so much time among the Gentiles that he had lost his ardent desire for the salvation of his people, the Jews. As we meditate on what God has done for us in Jesus Christ, we find ourselves stirred to similar concern for the lost.

Second, Paul the faithful apostle was only repeating what the Lord Himself had said. When Jesus encountered pride and unbelief, He often referred to God's merciful dealings with the Gentiles, both past (Luke 4:25–27) and future (Luke 13:22–30). He died for all, and He wants the Gospel to be proclaimed to all (Luke 24:45–47). Even today, for one and all, this fact stands true: Christ died for you. Your sins are forgiven.

And third, what Paul previously had written to the Roman Christians was an open secret: Because salvation had gone out to the Gentiles, maybe this reality would in turn make the Jews jealous (Romans 11:11). Paul wanted the Jews to inquire about Christ, even if they were driven at first by an inferior motive. "Now if their trespass brought riches for the world, and if their failure brought riches for the Gentiles," Paul wrote of the Jews, "how much more will their fullness bring!" (Romans 11:12).

We have seen that God truly acts in mysterious and surprising ways. He worked out His saving intention in Christ despite and even by way of sinful human blindness. He nudged the church toward the Gentiles through the outbreak of bloody persecution. He also turned the persecutor Saul, of all people, into the preacher and apostle Paul. So if the Jews' trespass and failure in rejecting Jesus and His Gospel brought riches for the Gentile world, this showed once more the abundance of God's grace in Christ. Jews too can receive this love and forgiveness from God through the Gospel.

The Power of God

The God who gave His Son as a ransom for all was not finished reaching out to the Jews or to anyone else. For his part, Paul would constantly proclaim the Gospel to everyone he could (28:30–31), both to the Jews and the many Gentiles in Rome. This Gospel remained the power of God unto salvation, revealing God's righteousness from faith to faith both to Jews and to Gentiles (Romans 1:16–17).

This Gospel was all the church had then or has today as a mission tool—but it was and it is more than enough. One theologian wrote these words about Acts:

> The only means the apostles know to carry out the work that Christ has given them to do is the Gospel. They have a mighty confidence in the effectiveness of the Gospel under all conditions and circumstances; they face people who are friendly and are willing to listen, and they tell them the Gospel-story; and they face howling mobs, who drag them out to stone them, and they tell them the Gospel-story; the jailer who was narrowly saved from committing suicide, and the governor who for two years hopes to extort a bribe, and the king who feels uncomfortable and would rather not have listened ... and the adulteress who has almost forgotten how to blush, they must all hear the same story. *(Hoyer, p. 30)*

This Gospel—this story of Christ and His work—packs all the power of the living God.

Launching Pad

For two years Paul lived in Rome in the place he had rented. No doubt the surroundings could have been better. Still, the apostle received everyone who came to him. And while under arrest and awaiting trial, he preached God's kingdom and taught about the Lord Jesus Christ with all boldness. No one tried to stop him (28:30–31).

This is the reason Paul's voyage to Rome proved so important. The empire's capital city was a center not only of governmental power, but also for trade and communications. "All roads lead to Rome" was more than just a saying. It was true. Rome became a great launching pad to other places for the Gospel. From this city, it could touch the lives of still more people. No wonder Acts describes Paul's progress to Rome, and the Lord's watchful care over him, in such vivid detail.

It must have delighted Paul particularly to report to the Philippians that the message of Christ had reached the members of the Praetorian guard (Philippians 1:13). Wherever these soldiers traveled on future assignments, they would take the Word with them. Paul's confinement in Rome turned into a profound blessing for the progress of the Gospel (Philippians 1:12).

No matter who we are, where we may be, or what adversities we may face, there is someone right where we are who needs to hear the Gospel. He or she can hear it from you. And that person can tell it to someone else, who can tell someone else, who can tell someone else … Who knows how far the love of God in Christ can go in this way?

It can go to the ends of the earth.

Summary

This journey through Acts has come full circle. Let's take a quick look at the ground we have covered.

We began by noting the ending as well as the beginning. In the process we glimpsed Christ continuing His saving work by preaching and teaching through Paul in Rome. As we said in chapter 1, the note on which the Acts narrative concludes is most fitting.

We gave attention to internal organization, especially in Acts 1:8: "You will be My witnesses in Jerusalem, and in all Judea and Samaria, and to the ends of the earth." By the end of Acts, as we have seen, the Gospel was ready to go out from the apostle Paul and the church at Rome to any point on the compass—to the ends of the earth.

Something about the Gospel message keeps it moving to new places, constantly drawing in new people. We focused on this fact when we examined two events repeated in Acts—the conversion of Paul and the story of Peter and Cornelius. Both are filled with implications for mission to the Gentiles. Both have their roots in justification by grace for Christ's sake through faith. Full and free salvation in Christ is the impetus that keeps the Gospel going out to all. Thus, we recommit ourselves to keeping the message straight and getting the message out.

Studying key words and ideas, we saw that it is the Holy Spirit who places the Lord's saving name on people to make them followers of the true Way—Jesus the Christ. After Him, we are called Christians. We were further reminded that spreading the Gospel occurs through Christians, despite the sins and flaws of Peter, Paul, you, or me.

We saw how the early Christians handled doctrinal controversy and personal conflict. We followed the Lord's work as Paul and his companions faced unexpected twists and found themselves in instances both of anger and opposition and of love and support. Of course, these features characterize our Christian lives too.

Finally, we traced in great detail Paul's path, through a variety of trials, from Jerusalem to Rome. The apostle was able to speak of the crucified, risen, and ascended Christ "with all boldness, unhindered" at the imperial capital (28:31). The message that had begun at Jerusalem, the city where the gospel according to St. Luke started (Luke 1:5ff) and ended (Luke 24:52–53), had come to Rome as the story continued in the companion volume, Acts.

The End?

But the interesting and thrilling part is that even when we reach the end of Acts, we do not come to the end of the story. As we said at the beginning of our trip through Acts, by the grace of God this is a story in which you and I are privileged to participate. Jesus is still doing and teaching through His church. What a great blessing from our God!

The story that began in Palestine continued through Rome in St. Paul's day, Wittenberg in Luther's, and Chicago in 1847. In that year, a small band of pastors and laypeople from a handful of congregations organized into a church body. Now the story comes to us. In this the 150th anniversary year of The Lutheran Church—Missouri Synod, we celebrate this story and ask God that through us it may continue to go out to the ends of the earth. Yes, *to the ends of the earth*.

Truly, this is the story with the happiest of endings.

Epilog

When my wife, Jean, and I were preparing to move to St. Louis in 1992, we decided the time had come to sell our dear old travel trailer. It did not seem possible that 26 years had passed since we purchased it. It was still in good condition. We had spent so many good times in it, first with the children and then by ourselves. The thought of parting with it was not easy to accept. There were so many good memories tied to it.

As I realized we were coming to the conclusion of our journey through Acts, I wanted you to know that our journey together has generated some good memories for me. Thumbing through my Bible, I began thinking, remembering, and even dreaming. Several thoughts crossed my mind.

Prayer

First, I considered the many passages in Acts that point to the important place prayer occupied in the early church. I was reminded how crucial prayer should continue to be among God's people. Paging through Acts again, I listed 24 direct references to prayer, plus several other indirect references to the dynamic power of prayer.

In many cases prayers were offered in time of crisis and need. At other times, prayers were coupled to the gathering of God's people in worship. Prayers often were connected with the church's mission and ministry in the world. The Christians in Acts devoted themselves to prayer in an ongoing way.

As I looked through the various passages, I thought of the important role prayer has played in my life and in the lives of those I have met. In the many types of situations we face, what a blessing it is to approach our God in prayer on a daily basis.

People

Second, I recalled the sale of our travel trailer. While we were sad about parting with our "home away from home," the Lord had a unique solution. The family to whom we sold the trailer reminded us of ourselves some 25 years earlier: a dad, a mom, and three small children. Like those early days for us, they did not have the money for extended vacations that involved motel stays and eating out. How excited they were to have a travel trailer for transportation. Jean and I talked about this as we watched them hook up the trailer, pull it out of the driveway, and head down the street. The travels would continue.

In our journey through Acts, perhaps we have grown more familiar with some of the first-century followers of our Lord. But as we have seen, the church's story did not end with the last verse of Acts. People have followed the Lord since, they follow Him today, and others will follow the Lord to the end of time. All followers move in one unending parade of believers, carrying the saving Gospel of Christ to the ends of the earth. The journey continues.

You know many fellow saints, and I do too. I thought back to the many people and congregations with whom I have worked. With them I shared many journeys through the Scriptures and through life, under the Lord's blessing. They were people who, like me, had come to know the glory of the Lord and the power of His saving Gospel. Together we remembered our baptisms, and together we knelt to receive the body and blood that bought and paid for our salvation.

Many of these dear Christian people have gone to be with our living Lord. Others continue the joyous journey of carrying the Gospel of Christ to the ends of the earth, especially to their little corner of it. Truly, the work and message of our Lord goes on.

Prospect

As I continued to reflect, I had what you might call a vision for the future. It was a mental image of that mass of people yet to join us in this remarkable journey. These are people who, by the grace of God, will come to faith in the years ahead. The most important person in Acts, our Lord Jesus Christ, continues to do and teach things in this world. As His Holy Spirit works by the power of His Word, Jesus still touches the hearts of men and women. In their lives these people too will continue to carry the saving Gospel to the ends of the earth. They will strive to live their faith in view of the eternity yet to come.

Promise

As you continue journeying through the Scriptures and journeying through life toward our heavenly home, I am sure that your trip will take you on all sorts of roads. Like other Christians, including those described in Acts, I always have found things easier when the Lord leads me on the interstate highways of life rather than on the gravel roads or the muddy ones. But I find it most important always to remember and cherish His promise. The footsteps of His presence, His forgiveness and blessing, have always been beside mine, even if they could not be seen with my human eyes.

In Christ, our good and gracious God gives this promise to you on your journey through life. Therefore, my heartfelt word for you is: God bless always! God bless mightily!

Praise

For all this we must and will ever say, God be praised! Yes, God be forever praised.

To Him who is able to keep you from falling and to present you before His glorious presence without fault and with great joy—to the only God our Savior be glory, majesty, power and authority, through Jesus Christ our Lord, before all ages, now and forevermore! Amen. *(Jude 24–25 NIV)*

Discussion Questions

You can use these study questions alone or in a class setting. Either way, they will help you summarize and apply what you have read in this book. The questions are arranged according to the sections of this book. Each set of questions covers one section. Each will cast a glance back, therefore, to one suggestion for Bible reading and how we employ it on our journey through Acts.

If you use these questions for group discussion, ask the members of your group to read the appropriate section of the book and the corresponding portion of Acts *before* you gather. It will take a minimum of 60 minutes to cover one set of questions. If you cover one section of the book each session, it will take you nine sessions to move through this material.

If you cannot meet for a full hour, or if your group discussion really takes off, it might be a good idea to take two sessions to cover one set of questions. This will extend the study to 18 weeks.

Section A

PAY ATTENTION TO THE BEGINNING AND THE ENDING

1. Why is it important to pay attention to the beginning and the ending of a book?

2. Summarize the answers to the *who, where, when, what,* and *why* questions in chapter 1.

3. What provides continuity in the church's history? Why is this continuity important?

4. How does it help us when we recall that the work of establishing the kingdom remains Christ's?

5. What myth about Acts and about Christ's ascension is identified in chapter 2? How can this myth contaminate the teaching of the Christian church?

6. Describe two ways this myth can be proven false. What comfort can we find in the truths that stand against the myth?

7. How does the ascension set the tone not only for the book of Acts, but also for our Christian lives today?

8. How was the Word of God prominent when the Holy Spirit came on Pentecost (Acts 2)?

9. What can we learn and apply to our lives from the "Pentecost prophecy" Peter quoted from Joel?

10. What did Peter say about Jesus in his Pentecost sermon? About his hearers? How do these things apply to us?

11. Why is the work of the Holy Spirit important to you?

Section B

Pay Attention to Internal Organization

1. Describe the organization of Acts, based on the hint given in Acts 1.

2. How is the word *witness* used in Acts? Cite examples.

3. Are we witnesses in this sense? Is this a good thing? Why?

4. Describe the shape of the early church's life in the Lord. Is it ours too? Why or why not?

5. Why is it important for the church that God has not only given us a Gospel to proclaim but also official proclaimers to announce it?

6. What can we learn from the early church about bearing up under persecution?

7. How did the Lord finally get the church to move beyond Jerusalem? What lesson does this account contain for us?

8. How can the apparent contradiction between Acts 2:38 and Acts 8:14–17 be resolved? What is the significance of this not only for the early church, but also for us?

9. What encouragement can we draw from the story of Philip and the Ethiopian?

Section C

PAY ATTENTION TO WHAT IS REPEATED

1. Why should we pay attention to what is repeated? Cite a personal example when this suggestion proved important.

2. Which two events are repeated in Acts? How often are they repeated?

3. What importance did Paul's conversion have for mission to the Gentiles?

4. What does the account of Paul's conversion in Acts, and his comments on it in the epistles, teach us about justification by grace for Christ's sake through faith?

5. Describe the story of Peter and Cornelius and its significance for the early church's outreach to the Gentiles.

6. How does the story of Peter and Cornelius emphasize the importance of justification by grace?

7. Why is it difficult for us to reach out to everyone with the Gospel? What help does the Gospel itself give us with this problem?

8. Why do we think of justification by grace as the other side of the coin of mission to the Gentiles? What are the implications for the church today?

9. Why must justification by grace remain the cornerstone of our faithfulness to God's Word?

Section D

PAY ATTENTION TO KEY IDEAS AND WORDS

1. How can you use Bible concordances? Why are these uses important for Bible study?

2. Which words should you look up in a concordance?

3. In Baptism, God put His name on you. How does it help you to know what His name means?

4. Why is the term "the Way" an especially good one to refer to the Christian faith?

5. What is the background of the word *Christian* as described in Acts? Is it a good name for God's people? Why or why not?

6. What does Acts tell us about the relationship between the Holy Spirit and Jesus Christ? What devotional significance does this relationship have for you?

7. Summarize the work of the Holy Spirit in the church as described in Acts. How does the Holy Spirit continue to work in the church today?

8. What difficulties were presented by the "disciples" whom Paul met at Ephesus (Acts 19)? What constructive lessons can we learn from this account?

9. Summarize the Holy Spirit's work.

Section E

PAY ATTENTION TO IMPORTANT CHARACTERS AND THEIR ACTIONS

1. Why is it important to understand what is meant—and not meant—as we apply to Acts the principle *pay attention to important characters and their actions?*

2. Give a character summary of Peter, based on passages in Acts. Supplement it with what you know about him from the gospels.

3. In their preaching, Peter and Paul both emphasized prophecy and fulfillment. Why?

4. The resurrection of Christ was important to Peter. What importance does it hold for us?

5. Does Acts show that Peter and Paul agreed or disagreed? Why is this meaningful?

6. Describe Paul's first recorded sermon. How is good preaching today like this sermon?

7. What can we learn about conversion from the reactions to Paul's preaching as reported in Acts?

8. Paul said, "We are men, like you in every way." Why should we take these words to heart?

9. Why do you think Acts devotes so much attention to Peter and Paul?

10. How can you see the importance of a character by the way he (or she) is tested?

Section F

PAY ATTENTION TO CONFLICTS

1. How is the suggestion to *pay attention to conflicts* related to the previous one about *paying attention to important characters and their actions?*

2. Cite passages in Acts that show not everyone in the early church was happy with mission to the Gentiles. How can Christians grow to love the revealed will of God and so grow to love other people?

3. Why was the apostolic council such a momentous event? How might things be different today if it had ended differently?

4. What are the two ways to evaluate theological

teaching? How were they used in Acts 15? How can we use them today?

5. Discuss this statement: We can convince ourselves that many errors are compatible with the Gospel if we lose sight of how the Gospel is taught in Scripture.

6. How can we profit from the example of the apostolic council?

7. List some other problems the first-century church had as discussed in Acts. How does such knowledge help us with problems the modern church faces?

8. Describe the early relationship between Paul and Barnabas. What may have caused the conflict over Mark?

9. What can the modern church learn from the way Paul and Barnabas handled their disagreement?

Section G

PAY ATTENTION TO UNEXPECTED TWISTS

1. Think of a situation in which the principle *pay attention to unexpected twists* is applicable to a narrative of fact, not fiction. Why is this principle helpful?

2. What was the significance of Paul's circumcision of Timothy? What lesson does it teach us?

3. Paul wanted to go to Ephesus or Bithynia, but the Spirit would not allow him. Why is the Spirit's guidance of Paul at this point important for us?

4. Summarize the turns of events that involved Paul at Philippi. What was the greatest twist of all?

5. Why is it good for Christians to recall that their faith is God's gift?

6. Why was Paul so concerned about the Thessalonians? What implications can we draw from this for the life of the modern church?

7. The Bereans were "more noble." How can we follow in their footsteps?

8. What can we learn about evangelism from Paul's speech at Athens? What can we learn about catechesis? About worship?

9. How did the Lord comfort Paul as the apostle faced the great challenge at Corinth? How does He comfort us as we face the challenge to meet people where they are but not leave them there?

Section H

PAY ATTENTION TO COMMON HUMAN EXPERIENCES

1. How can *paying attention to common human experiences* help us read narrative accounts?

2. Why was Ephesus so important to Paul and to the account in Acts of the third missionary journey?

3. Why is it essential that we pay attention to bringing the Gospel to people who are not "like us"?

4. What evidence do we have, from Acts and from elsewhere in the Bible, that Paul's work at Ephesus was difficult?

5. How does the Lord equip us to face the anger and opposition with which the world confronts the church today?

6. How is Paul's love for the pastors and the church at Ephesus evident in his speech in Acts 20?

7. How does Paul's speech in Acts 20 provide a model for pastors?

8. The Holy Spirit makes men pastors. What implications does this fact have for the modern church?

9. Discuss this statement: The Lord sends pastors for His church for the sake of the Gospel.

Section I

Pay Attention to Action Described in Detail

1. Why is it good advice to *pay attention to action described in detail?* Why is this especially important for reading the Scriptures?

2. Cite some parallels between Paul and Christ that emerge in the last portion of Acts. What lessons may we find in these parallels?

3. How did Paul link Christ, the hope of Israel, and the resurrection of the dead? How is this link important to you?

4. Summarize Paul's trials, legal and otherwise, between the time he was arrested at the temple and his departure for Rome. How would you react to these delays and disappointments? How can Christians more effectively face delay and disappointment in this world?

5. How does the hand of God become increasingly prominent in the account of Paul's voyage to Rome? What does this tell us about the importance of Paul's arrival in Rome?

6. Paul told the Jews in Rome that "the Gentiles …
   will listen." Why did he say this? What should
   we bear in mind as we interpret these words?

7. Why does Acts devote so much space to the
   account of Paul's trip to Rome?